PRAYING
WITH
AN
ATHEIST

JOE JOHNSON

WESTBOW
PRESS®
A DIVISION OF THOMAS NELSON
& ZONDERVAN

WestBow Press books may be ordered through booksellers or by contacting:

WestBow Press
A Division of Thomas Nelson & Zondervan
1663 Liberty Drive
Bloomington, IN 47403
www.westbowpress.com
844-714-3454

ISBN: 978-1-9736-9943-9 (sc)
ISBN: 978-1-9736-9944-6 (hc)
ISBN: 978-1-9736-9945-3 (e)

Library of Congress Control Number: 2023909838

Print information available on the last page.

WestBow Press rev. date: 07/28/2023

DEDICATION

This Book is dedicated to the following:

Esther, my rock.

Ziggy, my future.

Jason, my inspiration.

Last but certainly not least, Christ, my savior.

ABOUT THE AUTHOR

Who is the Author? I am, obviously. However, in truth, you are. The person across from you is. Your dentist is. Your spouse is. Your parent, your kid, your sibling. My name is irrelevant...my perspective, experiences, relationships, and faith...that's what has authored this book. The name on the cover is only there because...well...a name had to be there, and that name at least ensured that my family would buy this. Yet, beyond that...this book could have been written by anyone; and has been written by many in journals, diaries, prayer circles, meetings, texts, conversations, and confessionals.

The name on the cover is not important; you will see I am no Twain, Lewis, etc. I was raised Catholic, stepped away for a while, and found my faith restored in the wake of tragedy.

I am a husband, a father, a son, a brother, a friend, a ministry leader, a lawyer...and, for the time being, the author.

CONTENTS

INTRODUCTION

If Praying with an Atheist is a great title, it's an even better practice. I know it seems like an oxymoron, and I pray you know what that means, as the vocabulary doesn't get much easier from here. Praying with an Atheist is an exercise in acknowledging that all we want is for life as we know it to improve. It is a simple gesture of a common goal to see a fundamental shift of humanity toward decency.

So, you are an atheist and want to see if this is insulting or demeaning to your core beliefs or lack thereof. We will get to that. Or, you are a person of faith intrigued by the idea of converting an atheist. Or maybe you just needed something to read on the plane or commute to work. Or you got this from the library (in which case you are cheap and should buy a copy; I have kids to feed) and figured you'd try it. Irregardless...is not a word. Let us press on together.

This book is designed to provide information and motivation to the readers. It is sold with the understanding that the publisher is not engaged to render any psychological, legal, or any other kind of professional advice. The content of this book is a matter of opinion and is the sole expression and opinion of its author and not necessarily that of the publisher.

What kind of book is this? Truth be told, I am not really sure. Is it a book on faith? I guess, but it is not a Bible Study or even a Christian Lifestyle book. It is just a series of questions and an exploration of proffered answers. My friend called it a "self-help" book for those struggling with Faith. Self-Help…how can anybody give you advice on how to help yourself? This is not a self-help book; please don't expect any psychobabble or pearls of wisdom. There will be no inspirational quotes that you will see on posters in therapist and guidance counselor offices. This is not a warm and fuzzy book to make you feel good about yourself. It is questions about the world we find ourselves in, examination of those questions, and my novice answers. Ultimately, it is just perspective, and we have already addressed that I am irrelevant. So, why the book? Because it invites you to develop your perspective. It invites you to examine these issues with me, to agree or disagree. Go ahead, scream at the pages; I assure you, I won't get upset. It is a simple book. No flowery language. No positive messages. It is cold, calculating, and, to some, it can be, at times, offensive. Yet, it comes from a heart of truth, and I have always thought that when the truth is offensive, the offended need to examine their actions themselves, not the offender. The title is not misleading.

Before I sat to write this all down, I spoke with a good friend who is an atheist, and they said, "I pray that this all works out." It was March 2020, and COVID-19 had brought New York to a screeching halt. My friend had been out of work for a few weeks. This person had always made a point to express that they were a "Devout Atheist," ...an interesting self-proclaimed label. Yet, that day, they said they were "praying" that it all works out, not just for themselves but for friends, family, neighbors, and strangers. On that day, I *prayed with an atheist*. That is not a metaphor. No layered meanings there. It is just what happened.

Is this book really appropriate for you? I am hardly impartial, but I say YES. How can a Christian book be for everyone? Well, it is a Christian perspective, not a Christian book. Questions are posed and examined, cross-examined, evidence evaluated, opposition spoken to, and a conclusion is reached. It is a book for everyone because the issues involve everyone. Now when I say this is a book for everyone, there are no nursery rhymes, so be smart about it. Everyone means that people of all backgrounds should examine these questions. This book is for you because you did judge this book by its cover, and either you are or want to pray with an atheist.

Please do not shy away from it because of my Christian perspective. Will I quote the Bible? Well, I am writing this chronologically, so this Introduction is first, so at this juncture, I cannot affirmatively say one way or another. However, based on my notes and the topics outlined, I will quote scripture a few times, but not like a Biblical Concourse. I will also quote historical figures, other faiths, viewpoints, etc.; this book examines several core issues that affect us as human beings collectively. It will start with distinctly Christian issues to help build a foundation of my perspective and include some other macro issues.

Much of this book will contain transcripts of conversations with myself and an Atheist. This Atheist was interested in participating in an ALPHA Course I was hosting, as I regularly do. ALPHA is an amazing course that addresses everything discussed herein in far better detail and with much more intelligent people than I. This Atheist has since joined one of these courses, but this book comprises notes from our many lunches before they agreed to join. I wholeheartedly suggest that you research if there is a local ALPHA Course by you and participate; they are free and have food, so... why not? My Atheist friend was happy to help me with this project but did not want their name used. So, Avery Atheist is who will be seen in the transcripts, a nice gender-neutral name. Avery happens to start with "A," as does Atheist, so alliteration should be on our side to make this easy to follow.

I hope you enjoy this journey we will take together over the following few pages. I hope you are intrigued, and I hope you are entertained. I hope that you get something out of this. I hope you find some of it helpful. I hope you find some of it enlightening. Ultimately, I pray this book serves you well in some way...because in this rat race of life, we are all in it together, and I pray we all make it to the finish line a little better than rats.

So, here we go.

WHAT IS THE MEANING OF LIFE?

I figured we should start with a light, easy topic, nothing that people haven't struggled with for ages. You know, like the meaning of life. How many of us live Groundhog Day? We get up; we get dressed; we go to work; we go home; we do it again. Too often, we wish away our life. We can't wait until the weekend or our next vacation or day off. We hurry through the mundane to fly right through that time we so desperately wanted just to do it all over again and again and again. Why? What is the point?

Me: So, what is the point of life?

Avery: I think it is to live a good life.

Me: That's a wonderfully vague response.

Avery: True; I guess "good" is subjective.

Me: Sure is.

Avery: I guess what I mean by that is to leave the world a little better than how I found it.

Me: That's it?

Avery: I guess.

Me: A lot of guessing going on.

Avery: Ok, so what's the point?

Me: Life.

Avery: What?

Me: The point of life is life. The real question is, what is the purpose; what is my purpose in this life? That you have to decide on your own.

Avery: And what psalm is that in?

Me: Based on context clues…all of them.

There must be more to life than this

There must be more to life than this

I live and hope for a world filled with love

Then we can all just live in peace

There must be more to life, much more to life

There must be more to life, more to life than this

OK, now reread that with the author's voice belting it in your head, and I promise it is far more moving. That is from the song, *There Must Be More to Life Than This,* from the 1985 album Mr. Bad Guy, written and performed by the late, great Freddie Mercury. I opine that Mr. Mercury nailed it in that verse, a world filled with love and a life of peace. Isn't that the point? Yet, let us look at the song's history. It was initially recorded in 1981 as a duet between Freddie and Michael Jackson. The duet was not released until after Mr. Jackson's death, but the fact that this song was recorded as a duet by these men is something else. Well, I am not big on coincidences. Both these men were massive stars and amazing musical talents, and both were lauded as masters or "kings/queens" of the industry. Yet, both were haunted by their own personal demons, addictions, and darkness. No need to go into theories or conjecture against either one. Both men were celebrated as philanthropists and humanitarians in several respects. They were charitable and kind while also being self-tortured and lost. Rumors of darkness and ill will plagued them both. Nobody is spared from depression, fear, anxiety, or darkness. Celebrity suicides, overdoses, etc. serve as grim reminders that those who "have it all" still seek some purpose in life, and when they cannot find it, they can succumb to that negativity.

I agree with Avery; we want to leave this world better than how we found it. Does that mean we should recycle? Does that mean I should buy an electric car? Or does it mean feeding the hungry, donating blankets for the homeless, etc.? Is it any one thing? Is there a way to make the world a better place? In John 14:6 ESV, Jesus says, *"I am the way and the truth and the life."* Pretty straightforward for me. Yet, maybe not so clear for Avery.

Avery: So, are you saying that being a Christian is the only way to have a good life?

Me: Not necessarily.

Avery: Then what are you saying?

Me: I am saying that it depends on what you call "good" ...there are plenty of morally sound non-Christians.

Avery: And plenty of immoral Christians.

Me: No...

Avery: Blowing up clinics, attacking and killing homosexuals...these are moral actions?

Me: No...but they're not Christians.

Avery: They believe in and follow Jesus.

Me: Both you and Jeffrey Dahmer grew up believing in Santa, yet you both have different cookbooks...belief is not enough...to be a Christian, you have to follow Christ, and that requires forgiveness and love...those people do not follow Christ.

Avery: So, are you a Christian?

Me: I'm trying to be.

Any Christian who speaks with moral superiority and judgment just does not get it. It's like that guy who owns a bunch of camo, wears *semper fi* on all his clothing, and goes shooting all the time but was never enlisted. Owning the uniform does not make you a soldier, and those who impersonate are far more offensive than those who outwardly oppose. Christianity is not a state of being; it is a journey. For those who choose that journey, it provides purpose and meaning to their lives.

400 B.C. Socrates birthed the philosophical ideology that the meaning of life was present pleasure; this concept grew into what is commonly known as Cyrenaic doctrine. Aristippus took Socrates' theory and expounded it to the extreme. He believed that a person should do whatever made them happy at that moment and that planning for the future was an exercise in futility. Such an ideology stresses the importance of physical pleasure and is centered entirely on the self. Truth is subjective, knowing others is impossible, relationships are vapid, and social norms are archaic. The meaning of life is to do whatever pleases you at the moment. Such an ideology laughs in the face of the concept of sin. It promotes selfishness and disregards the common good. Could life really be all about what makes us happy right here and now? If so, we revert to the question of celebrity suicides. Is it that society does not allow us to adopt this doctrine? Are we inherently selfish at the core?

Me: Are people inherently out for just themselves?

Avery: I don't think we can answer that.

Me: Why not?

Avery: Because I don't think it is a generalized issue; I think some people are, but not people in general.

Me: Ok...so you would agree that the meaning of life cannot be to do whatever makes you happy.

Avery: Definitely...otherwise, I'd die in a hot tub with Reese's.

So, while the Greeks in 400 B.C. claimed "Me, Me, Me" was the secret of life, that was not the only ideology birthed at the time. In China, Mo Di developed a philosophical doctrine that called for the exact opposite. According to Mohism, the meaning of life is total equality; only when everyone shows the same amount of care, concern, and contribution to the wellbeing of everyone else can purpose truly be found. Wealth, happiness, health, and pleasure should be equally distributed to honor the desires of the divine so that everyone may reap the benefits in the afterlife. Can the meaning of life indeed be that your life has no meaning individually? That you are irrelevant as an independent person?

These are historical extremes of philosophical ideologies birthed simultaneously from different regions. Yet, they are far from the only answers to our question about the meaning of life. Cynicism as a philosophical ideal, and not just a late-night talk show gimmick, is also birthed from Socrates' teachings. Cynics strive to live a moral existence within society. Cynics practice "parrhesia," which is truth speaking to break immoral societal norms. Truth is big. However, Cynicism does not stop at truth-speaking; to them, the meaning of life was self-sufficiency. They are turning away from relationships and basic comforts and abandoning possessions and people to be entirely self-reliant. That was the point of life.

Tibetan philosophy is akin to the Buddhist religion in that the purpose of our existence is to end the world's suffering.

You can be centered on self and remove suffering in your small circle, or you can take on the suffering of others. This ideology is an interesting one as it is a positive reflection with a core of suffering and pain. Tibetans have specific rules and regulations on how to rid the world of suffering through understanding the nature and cause of suffering, but at the end of the day, they believe that the meaning of life is to end suffering. We have all seen the videos of monks lighting themselves on fire. Sacrifice, martyrdom, and suffering are not unique concepts to Tibetans, but how they exercise these concepts and deal with them is unique. Many would say that we are the cause of the suffering, and what causes one person to suffer may benefit another. The complexity of human relations makes the ending of suffering a lofty goal.

Aztecs were basically Jedi; they believed in "teotl," the invisible force connecting all things. Not a deity but an energy, and they firmly believed that the meaning of their life was to protect and pass that force on to future generations. They lived a life of balance in an attempt to protect "teotl" and honor the cyclical nature of existence.

Darwinism is different from evolution, while the doctrines are related based on the teachings and ideologies of Charles Darwin. The core of Darwinism is that DNA is to be passed on and that the purpose of life is to sustain life for future generations and pass on our genetics. Avery and like-minded persons are always so quick to play the Darwin card. However, Darwin's seminal work, On the Origin of

Species, highlights that Darwin believed that God was the first Cause of life and that he was the one who set the laws of nature. It's ironic how Darwin's theories have been watered down to serve an agenda...it is like his ideologies have been forcibly "devolved."

Nihilism is perhaps the "best" explanation for the meaning of life because it makes me smile the most. Nihilism is the belief that nothing is valued and that there is no point to life or anything at all. Friedrich Nietzsche argued that nihilism would be the downfall of humanity. There is no truth; love does not exist, and happiness is an illusion. At its inception, Nihilists believed that destroying societal constructs to identify their meaningless nature was essential, but even that grew into indifference because it didn't really matter.

Epicurus came up with a fun philosophy that now bears his name. He believed in the duality of particles. Soul and Body, they could not exist without one another. The point is to maximize pleasure and minimize pain. However, he did have a "morality clause" of sorts. Where Aristippus said to do what you want to feel good right now, Epicurus acknowledged the concept of guilt and that doing "wrong" would negate the positive feeling and alter it to negativity, thereby diminishing your overall happiness and pleasure. Both believed that there is no eternal reward or damnation; the meaning of life was to make the most of the time you have because in the end...it is simply over.

Me: So, if there is no God, no afterlife, no eternal reward… then why live a good and morally sound life

Avery: Is it your faith that keeps you on the straight and narrow?

Me: Absolutely.

Avery: Then doesn't that make me the more moral person since I am not doing it for a reward?

Me: That is the mix-up; I do not live a moral existence for the reward; I acknowledge that I cannot earn my way into the reward

Avery: Then why do it?

Me: Because I have already received the reward

Avery: What?

Me: For me, it is not a checklist of good deeds to get a golden ticket

Avery: That is exactly what it is.

Me: That is the misunderstanding of Christianity…you see, no deed I do can earn my way into the reward…I was born a sinner, and I acknowledge that no matter how hard I try, I will die a sinner.

Avery: Then what is the point?

Me: Grace.

Avery: Grace…ohh…she passed away 30 years ago.

While I laughed at the pop culture reference (I hope you get it), my point remains that my reward is not earned or gained...it was given...through grace. Accepting grace is no easy feat. Many like to pretend that if they were handed an elaborate gift, they would gladly accept it. Yet, the truth is that unprompted gifts make many people, me included, uncomfortable; why? Well, we feel we didn't do anything to deserve it, we have nothing to give in return, and that unworthiness is heavy. So, "Divine Grace" is the heaviest gift for a believer. The concept is not strictly Judeo-Christian; the idea of "Divine Grace" exists across many beliefs. This grace gives eternal life, sanctifies, inspires, protects, strengthens, and connects us. Abstract as it may be, most people on earth acknowledge and relate to the doctrine of "Divine Grace." Then again, most people on Earth once believed that the world was flat...and now many do again...which is another story. The idea of "unmerited favor" is one that anybody can relate to, favor and provision provided to those with no claim or reason to receive it. That is what "Divine Grace" is: an explanation or label for God's unmerited favor toward humanity, the ultimate gift. That is the Point of Life, to live fully in the Grace given to us.

When Paul went to Athens (Paul, an Apostle and follower of Christ who is credited with writing many Christian texts) to tell the people of the good news of Christ and His resurrection, he was received by a not always accepting audience. Some mocked and laughed at him. I've been there. I used to laugh at religious zealots as a self-proclaimed intellect, but I still do sometimes. The absurdity of it all seemed laughable. However, I have come to learn that I was not ready to learn at that time. Avery and I engage in respectful and meaningful dialogue, but that is not always the case. Some people view themselves as intellectual superiors and believe that anyone who lives a life of faith must be intellectually inferior to them. That is a person who has most definitely not accepted grace. Neil Kensington Adam, the brilliant British chemist, was a Christian, as was the founder of the Braille Institute of America, and Dr. John Billings, the list can go on and on. The truth is that any side can point to an elite group of intellectuals to highlight that they are not intellectually inferior, which in fact, proves my point that the existence of faith is not an indication of intellectual inferiority. Anyone who believes otherwise is an intellectually inferior individual. Appreciate the irony in that statement for a moment.

While many mocked and jeered at Paul, others felt convicted and believed. They heard the call and answered immediately. An invitation to a personal relationship with Christ sounds perfect, peaceful, freeing, and loving. It is beautiful, annoying for those of us not engaged in that sort of deep love relationship, but beautiful just the same.

Then some listened, unsure but curious. That is most people I meet, and if I am completely honest, the most relatable reactions to the "good news." Questioning, examining, and doubting are not an absence of faith but an exploration of it. Grace gives us that ability; Grace employs us with the necessary tools to examine Faith.

The question *What Is The Meaning Of Life* cannot be answered in a few short pages for all of humanity. Yet, for me, it can be answered in just one word "Grace." I have love in my life, I have existed in the same time as David Bowie, and I have experienced great joy and loss. I have done nothing to deserve the blessings I have received. Nihilists say nothing matters – take from them the ability to not dwell on negativity. Cynics value the truth, something we should all learn to do, speak the truth with love. Mo Di gave the world Mohism to bring about equality, lift up your neighbors and be charitable. Aristippus was extreme, but do not ignore yourself and enjoy pleasures, learn to live in the moment. Tibetans are right; we do want to end all suffering. Darwin was on to something when he called for us to improve with each generation. Epicurean philosophy teaches us to value friendships and interpersonal relationships. The Aztecs showed us that we are all connected, and that life is not finite.

The level of detail in a single snowflake, or the cellular structure of a leaf, is so intricate and beautiful, and they serve rudimentary and singular fleeting purposes. Everyone one of us is different, and we will all prescribe different meanings to our lives. Painters, Poets, Mechanics, Intellectuals, Singers, Chefs, Parents, Children, Siblings, Teachers, Nurses... there is no right or wrong meaning to our lives. At the end of the day, there is no specific meaning for life that can be painted with a broad stroke. So, while we may not be able to state the meaning of life succinctly, we can say that life has meaning. The answer lies in the question itself. Your Life Has Meaning! You are not a mistake! You have a purpose! Your existence is a mathematical anomaly; your life is a gift.

Avery: So, what does grace have to do with the meaning of life?

Me: It is through Grace that I can accept that I have a specific purpose.

Avery: And what is that?

Me: I have no idea.

Avery: So, we are right where we started.

Me: I'm not.

Avery: How so?

Me: We started with "What is the point of life?"

Avery: Yeah, and we still have no answer.

Me: The point is life, and with grace, I know that life is a gift; I value the gift and look forward to figuring out how to use it.

Avery: Ok, so what is the point of my life?

Me: You, my friend, are valued and loved by someone you don't even know; luckily, they know you.

WAS JESUS
FOR REAL?

Yes...next chapter.

OK, perhaps we should take this a tad more seriously. The fact is that the existence of Christ is widely accepted among theologians, archeologists, historians, and scholars alike. For now, we will avoid Christian texts in examining Jesus' existence. Flavius Josephus was a Judaic scholar who wrote about the history of Judaism in 93 AD. In his writings, he has two specific references to Jesus. Fast forward 20 years, and we have the Romans Pliny and Tacitus' accounts. Tacitus details that Jesus was executed under the Roman prefect Pontius Pilate who oversaw Judea from 26-36 AD. His reports are consistent with gospel accounts. Pliny adds that in the region he served as governor (Northern Turkey), people worshipped the executed Jesus as a God. All these accounts do one thing very well, establish the true existence of Jesus.

People today debate the existence of Jesus, yet there are hundreds of firsthand accounts. Jesus' title of "messiah" and who signed the acknowledgment of paternity may be an issue, but his existence should not be. Even those who do not believe that Jesus is whom Christians claim he is acknowledge his existence. In early rabbinical writings, Jesus is identified as the illegitimate child of Mary and a Sorcerer. Pagan authors such as Lucian and the philosopher Celsus dismissed Jesus as a conman. Yet, you will be hard-pressed to find a denial of His existence in a historical context.

Avery: Can we be sure that Jesus really existed?

Me: I don't know about "we," … but I sure can.

Avery: Seriously, how can we be sure this is not a fantastical story made up to make people believe?

Me: Roman tax records.

Avery: What?

Now, Avery is highly educated and someone I respect immensely. That dialogue is not meant to disparage or insult Avery or anyone of a like mind. Pilate's tax records, census, rabbinical writings, and soldier accounts all these texts confirm that Jesus existed. The fact is that the existence of Christ has been tied to the Religion of Christianity for far too long. As people have challenged the legitimacy of the Church, they have challenged the legitimacy of Jesus' existence. Jesus is Jesus, and the Church is the Church. They can, are, and should be viewed as separate entities.

In 2017 approximately 40% of the adults in England reported that they did not believe Jesus was an actual historical figure. Philosopher Michel Onfray and others have argued that both Jesus and the city of Nazareth were constructs of Christianity. Then we have true historians debunking this pseudo-scholarly vein, such as Maurice Casey and Bart Ehram. The shroud of Turin, the theory that Jesus was the great-grandson of Cleopatra based on gold coins bearing His likeness, and many other theories exist. There are a lot of questionable archeological factors. However, the first-hand and subsequent written accounts of Judeo-Christian and Roman authors give us the best evidence that Christ did, in fact, exist. Archeologist and historian Byron McCane believe that not only do we know that Jesus existed, but that both the baptism and crucifixion of Christ are well documented and provable. The fact is that based on empirical, impartial, and historical data, there can be little to no reasonable doubt that Jesus did, in fact, live and was, in fact, crucified. I am not a historian, archeologist, or expert in any way. I am, however, literate, so if you need clarification on the existence of Jesus, put a bookmark here, do some research, and then come back. I am not talking about Resurrection or faith...not yet. I am simply saying that Jesus existed as a real person, and several non-Christian texts historically document that.

So, what about the Christian texts? First off, we must admit that they are conclusory and biased. However, we should examine the nature of that conclusion and bias. We call them "Christian" texts, copies of the gospels transcribed in many languages, Greek, Aramaic, etc., with several translations, hundreds more than any other text on earth. We call them "Christian" texts now, yet, when they were written, there was no "Christianity" as we have come to know it. In fact, these texts' existence has supported the foundation, development, and growth of Christianity.

In 1902 Walter Nash purchased a manuscript on papyrus. It contains the 10 Commandments from the Book of Exodus and the *Shema Yisrael* prayer from the Book of Deuteronomy. Many scholars believe that Egyptians used the papyrus as a prayer card in daily worship. It dates back to the second century. Then between 1947 and 1956, in Qumran near the Dead Sea came one of the most renowned archeological discoveries, commonly known as The Dead Sea Scrolls—every Book of the Old Testament except Nehemiah and Esther with manuscripts dating back to 250 BC. The Leningrad Codex was dated 1008 AD, and the discovery of The Dead Sea Scrolls showed scholars that the text had not substantively changed over the years; by "years," I mean centuries. These texts remained true to form for centuries. The Codex Sinaiticus is considered the first complete New Testament translation and dates back to the fourth century. The gospel of Mark has been identified on a parchment dating back to the first century. Hundreds of hand-transcribed gospels have been uncovered over the centuries, and they all conform with one another. This is a foundation of historical text that Christianity is built upon.

All of this goes to support that, *Yes, Jesus was for real.*

Avery: Ok, so even if Jesus was real, the whole crucifixion and resurrection thing seems a tad farfetched.

Me: No...not a tad farfetched...seems insane.

Avery: So, I win?

Me: I think we both know better than that...something seeming farfetched is not an indication of falsehood

Avery: Yeah, but you pride yourself on being pragmatic.

Me: Yes, I do.

Avery: And you are a man of logic...obnoxiously so at times.

Me: Also, true.

Avery: So, we are at this impasse.

Me: How so?

Avery: Occam's razor dictates that you cannot accept the resurrection story.

Me: Oh no...the exact opposite, actually.

Intellectuals of all pursuits often use Occam's razor to explain the simplicity of complex situations. The diluted version is that the "simplest answer is most often correct." However, William of Ockham was a Franciscan Theologian who combated the concept that Faith and Reason were diametrically opposed forces. This principle succinctly and accurately states that "entities should not be multiplied without necessity." His use of logic and reason was fundamental and, to this day, revered. Yet, he was an English Franciscan friar; ergo, he was a man of devout faith. The doctrine that so many intellects use to argue the validity of faith was, in fact, developed to defend the existence of divine miracles. So, in short, logic dictates that the resurrection is real.

Another great support for the resurrection is the lack of evidence. Meaning, where is the body? The existence of Jesus is well documented. The crucifixion is also well documented by secular and non-secular records. So, if Jesus, arguably the most significant human being to ever walk the earth, is real, and his death is well documented, then where is his body? Theories of grave robbers, body swaps, Church coverups, and cremation litter the skeptics. Grave robbers...if you have the body of Jesus, if you robbed his tomb, that discovery would be worth more than any other archeological find in modern history. Plus, the grave clothes, the only items of actual value at the time were left behind, folded. The robbing of Jesus' tomb would have brought fame and fortune and no doubt would not have gone undocumented. The body swap theory is laughable. The idea that Jesus' body was mixed up or exchanged with someone else's is borderline insane, as it does not answer the question, "Where is the body?" Swapping with another body means that the body would still be able to be found. Church coverup is one of the more intriguing theories; the story goes that the Catholic Church suppressed evidence of Jesus' body. Atheists and skeptics love this one. It has espionage and distrust of organized religion. The problem is…math. The creation of the Roman Catholic Church is from the Great Schism of 1054 or the Reformation of 1520, depending on whom you believe. Some say no, Constantine created the Church, well, not accurate, but even that would put us as approximately 300 A.D. So, where was the body all that time?

Five hundred people report seeing Jesus after his resurrection. Cremation, again, math. As the organization of a common "coverup" over that many people with just enough difference in recollection to support human error without the assistance of any social media or technological communication…well… that is far less believable than the resurrection. Then we have the idea that Jesus' body was cremated, again…math. Cremations are a relatively new idea, like 19th-century new. A cremation of Jesus would still have a skeleton and again beg the question…where is the body?

So, records indicate that Jesus existed. Firsthand accounts say that Jesus was resurrected. No logical alternative has presented any evidence to the contrary. There is no physical evidence to disprove or even argue against the resurrection. There is no reliable contrary historical data to proffer alternatives to the Christian ideology. The simplest explanation is that Jesus did exist, did die, and was resurrected. Why is that a problem?

Me: Why does the possibility of Jesus' resurrection scare you?

Avery: It doesn't...I just find it unbelievable.

Me: You cannot buy Coca-Cola in North Korea.

Avery: What?

Me: You could fit the entire world's population in L.A.

Avery: OK.

Me: More people visit France than any other country.

Avery: So?

Me: France Avery! France!

Avery: I know I will regret this...but...what is your point?

Me: Those are all inconceivably facts: no Coke in North Korea, everyone on earth crammed in L.A., and France is the number one destination...just because it sounds unbelievable and makes you nauseous doesn't make it untrue.

Avery: Ok...but those fun facts that make people look at you weirdly in social gatherings don't make people feel shame?

Me: Now I am lost.

Avery: If Jesus existed and was crucified for us, then our existence is one of shame.

Me:...ummm...you need therapy.

Avery: You know what countries cannot get Coca-Cola, but I need therapy.

Me: Shortlist North Korea and Cuba...but...to be fair, I learned that pre-Obama and have not followed up since, so it may have changed...I mean that Jesus has nothing to do with shame...instead of shame, you should feel liberty and gratitude...you should revel in the grace provided.

Avery: It just seems too fantastical to be real.

Shame. It is a big topic for all people, regardless of faith. The concept that "our existence is one of shame" means an acknowledgment that we are unworthy of such a sacrifice. That acknowledgment is the first step to acceptance of grace. This is not a matter of religion but of logic. If someone died for you because they want you to be saved from all the wrong choices you may make in your entire life, and they chose to be punished for those choices, shame is the natural response. It is so because we have no choice, if we are honest with ourselves, to recognize the fact that we are unworthy of such a sacrifice. The difference that comes with faith is that faith will turn that shame into the acceptance of grace. Lack of faith does not negate the understanding of Jesus' sacrifice; it helps reconcile it so that we need not hang our heads in shame; rather, we can lift our hearts with gratitude and grace.

Many of my friends, pastors, family, etc., have all tried to challenge atheists' disbelief, but that is a myth. It is not that atheists do not believe in God; it is that they do not know God. If you consider something to be true, that is a belief. However, when you accept a concept as truth, that is knowledge. True atheists will argue the lack of knowledge, the absence of knowing, that is the core of their "disbelief." Bats are not blind, camels do not store water in their humps, your blood is not color-changing based on oxygen, the earth is not flat, diamonds do not come from coal, and Jesus is real. These are truths; we may have learned things contrary; we may believe things contrary...but...truth is truth, and the truth is liberating...for more on that, see John 8:32. So yeah...Jesus is for real.

IF JESUS WAS WHOM CHRISTIANS SAY HE WAS, WHY DID HE DIE?

This is where it can get a tad theological, but I will break it down as simply as I can. Many priests, evangelists, pastors, parents, great aunts, etc., will tell you that Jesus died for all of mankind's sins. Well, while that may be true, He actually died for me. I cannot speak for you, but I know that He died for me. I have people whom I love deeply, and I would die for them, so Jesus' sacrifice is not all that confusing to me. True Christianity is not about religion; it is about relationships; it is about not just accepting Christ; it is about knowing him, laughing with him, crying to him, yelling at him, loving him, and being loved by him. Christianity is not about statues, rituals, candles, or prayers…it is about very real and very personal relationships.

In order to understand why Jesus would willingly sacrifice himself for just me, we can go to the playbook; we find the answer in Matthew 18:12-14 or Luke 15:3-7...you pick. That is where Jesus gives the parable of the shepherd who leaves his flock of ninety-nine sheep in order to find the one that is lost. The simple parable is how Jesus taught, using parables and short stories, open-ended with his message at the core. A shepherd with one hundred sheep notices that one has wandered off, so he leaves his herd to find the one and rescue it. Morality and logic cloud our minds because we are imperfect beings; as such, we criticize the shepherd for disregarding the ninety-nine. We haphazardly chastise the shepherd for choosing the welfare of one over the others. Yet, break it down. The ninety-nine are with the shepherd; they are safe, grazing, and accounted for. The one is lost and potentially in peril. Leaving the ninety-nine for the one only seems silly if you see yourself as the shepherd or part of the ninety-nine. Yet, if you humble yourself enough to realize you are the one, it is pretty awesome. Let's say you are at a park, just you and a hundred kids; you are playing catch, throwing a frisbee, pushing kids on swings, and having a great time. You notice a kid is missing. You shout the kid's name. Maybe you call for help. You do what is responsible and safe. What if the missing kid is your kid? It does not make the other ninety-nine less significant or important, but they are here, at the park, safe...your baby is missing. Are you so calm now? If we are truly honest with ourselves, we know that our love, devotion, and personal relationship will send us out in search of the one. That, to me, is the most significant point in the parable; the shepherd seeks the lost, not the other way around.

Avery: So, you claim that Jesus is God?

Me: Sure, do.

Avery: And that he turned water into wine?

Me: Yup.

Avery: Stopped a storm?

Me: Uh-huh.

Avery: And could basically do anything?

Me: Yes.

Avery: Yet, his ministry lasted a few short years, and he was captured and executed?

Me: Question?

Avery: Why didn't he stop his execution?

Me: For me.

Jesus acknowledges this confusion in the gospel of Matthew. In Matthew 26:53, he clearly states that he could call down legions of angels to rescue him. He makes it clear that God would send *Him* angels. That up to twelve legions of angels would be at *His* disposal. That if *He* just asked that *His* Father protect *Him* and that *He* would be saved. You see, Jesus could have stopped the crucifixion, he could have been saved...but we wouldn't have been. That is the foundation of Christianity. The Shepherd sacrificed his safety for the one; he chose to do so.

Free will is a thing. I'm not talking Garden of Eden...I am simply acknowledging the universally accepted view that we as human beings have the ability to make our own choices and exercise that ability regularly, and such exercise is called free will. People choose to do things that are on their faces illogical. Plea bargaining is the practice of striking a deal with the prosecution to get a lesser charge in hopes of lenient penalties. Too often, "not guilty" people accept pleas to things they are not guilty of in order to "make a deal" and avoid the gamble of their freedom. Logic dictates that an innocent person would not admit to guilt. My 9 to 5 tells me that people do exactly that all the time. Our entire Western society laughs in the face of logic; we perform services and provide goods for exchange of woven cotton paper with pictures of dead people on it; in fact, many of us don't even get that we get screens with numbers on it and don't even see the dead people paper. We do these things because of faith. We have faith in our system. Faith is a choice, as is the absence of it. What does this have to do with Why Did Jesus Die? He chose to. It does not need to make sense to you. It was His choice. Pure and simple. The fact is that if we accept that Jesus chose to die, we then are naturally drawn to "Why?"

Avery: If he had lightning strike his accusers and jumped off that cross and called down angels with swords, I think the vagueness and doubt would be wiped away.

Me: I suppose it would be.

Avery: So, why didn't your Jesus do that?

Me: Because he respected you too much.

Let's break this down. Avery is insinuating that his belief hinges on Jesus' performance. The problem is that Jesus' actions are a direct result of Avery's. If Jesus had acted like a Spartan General with winged soldiers at his back, then Avery would believe and would dutifully follow Jesus, but not by faith. That is the lynchpin. Hebrews 11:1 NIV says that *faith is confidence in what we hope for and assurance about what we do not see.* Jesus wants us to follow him because we have faith. If you have faith in digital transfers and the value of dead people's paper, how can you not have faith in a savior? Once again, Belief and Knowledge are at odds. Avery seeks knowledge, yet Jesus wants us to obtain knowledge but be guided by faith. 2 Corinthians 5:7 NIV says, *for we live by faith, not by sight.* Jesus wants you, me, Avery, and everyone to be found and to come to him, but of their own volition…he respects your will. Showing up with legions of armed angels is not an invitation of faith but a draft or military siege.

We started this by saying that it is about "relationships." If your spouse asks you to follow them as hundreds of guys behind them hold weapons in support of their will, that is an unhealthy relationship. Jesus is not an abusive boyfriend. He is a loving husband, protective father, and helpful brother…he is the perfect relationship for you, me, Avery, and everyone else. People confuse Church with Christ. Church is a collection of flawed sinners with a common faith. Christ is the shepherd still seeking the lost.

Why did He die? Because He could. Because He could die to save me. I've lashed out in anger, hurt people, sinned, and maybe you're better than me, but I know my shortcomings and am eternally grateful for the forgiveness and salvation I have undeservedly received. I WAS FOUND because I cried out to Him, and because He sacrificed himself, I am saved. I can appreciate the lack of clarity. I can see the mystery behind the question.

Me: Why do you think He died?

Avery: Because a Roman soldier drove a spear through him.

Me: Good.

Avery: Good, what?

Me: You acknowledge He died, which means He lived.

Avery: But his self-sacrifice still doesn't make sense to me, nor does it make him God.

Me: Well, you would die for your child(ren)?

Avery: Absolutely.

Me: Then it makes some sense to you...the sacrifice is made out of love...but as far as Him being God, that's not why He died; that is why He lives.

Avery: Yeah, it seems unfair that if I sacrifice myself for a loved one, I don't get to come back in three days.

Me: You are a hundred percent right.

Avery: I'm winning you over.

Me: You get to come back and be bathed in glory immediately if you follow Him, and He had to wait three days...so unfair.

The question "Why Did Jesus Die?" addresses the fact that He did die, and that is a big deal since the tomb was empty, and His body was never found. The Roman Empire did not want Jesus to be celebrated; they did not want Christianity to rise. They collected followers of Christ after the tomb was found empty and interrogated, tortured, and bribed them for the location of the body. No body was found or reported; all said that He had, in fact, risen, some even to the point of death. So, if we accept that Jesus did, in fact, die, the natural follow-up question is, "Why" did he die?

Romans 6:23 ESV answers that question succinctly, in that *the wages of sin is death*. I will admit that this is one of my favorite verses because of the simplicity of it. Not much interpretation is needed here as it leads the reader to comprehend the cost associated with sinful nature. This portion of scripture is written by a guy named Paul. Paul spent much time in jail and wrote many letters. Letters, for our post-80s babies, are correspondences written on paper, placed in envelopes, and mailed to the intended audience of that correspondence. When Paul wrote this, he had not yet visited the Roman church, yet, he knew that Rome as a city was vast and diverse, and he felt that his letter to the church in Rome must impart the importance of Christian values to be the foundation of the church. You see, Paul was...well...a huge cheerleader for Jesus. The letter to the church of Rome was written in approximately 58 A.D. This brief history lesson behind one verse is important because context is important. Almost 60 years after Jesus' death, Paul was writing letters to churches around the known world to convey the earnest nature of Jesus' loving act of self-sacrifice.

The wage of sin is death. That is an interesting phrase; words have meaning. Wage; why wage? Why not "cost" or something else? I mean, we work for a wage. This is not one of those "lost in translation" issues. In Greek manuscripts, the word is "opsonia," which translates directly to "wages." Ergo, this is a purposeful word choice, but why? We, collectively, as a people, actively seek wages whether we realize it or not. We go to work; we create a product; we perform a service; we expect to be paid. It is the same with sin, we get paid at the end of the day, and the payment is death. Paul uses the term "wages" because when we work, we expect to be paid what we deserve, what we have earned, and what is fair. So, through the work of sin, we get paid what we deserve, what we have earned, what is fair...a spiritual and physical death.

That is why Jesus chose to die. My sin. I started this by saying that He died for me. I am a sinner. Pure and simple, I have sinned probably ten times while typing this very sentence. I get angry. I have impure thoughts. I am an attorney. I am an attorney who focuses his practice on family law and divorces...ten may have been an understatement. The point is that I know I sin. I try not to. I try to stay on the straight and narrow for the most part. Yet, I fail miserably. I live a life of sin, and for it, I deserve death. Yet, Jesus took on my sin, and for it, he was killed; he accepted my payment.

It can be convoluted because many people say Jesus paid for our sins. While that is not wrong, I find it easier to understand this question by realizing that he received our just payment.

Avery: So, you're saying your chit was called in, and he covered you.

Me: I'm saying, who uses the word "chit" ...gamble much?

Avery: Ok, he paid your debt.

Me: No, my debt keeps building, so I don't look at it like that.

Avery: So, how do you look at it?

Me: I'm on death row, and I deserve it...and as they walk me to the gallows, Jesus jumps up there and yells, "Send that man to my palace; I accept his fate," and is killed in my place.

Avery: A tad dark, no?

Me: They have children's bibles...doesn't make it a children's book.

Jesus died for me. It is my fault. My sin and depravity are what Jesus died for. He knew the man I would be, my choices and the transgressions I would commit. He knew I deserved to die for my choices, and he took my place; that is why Jesus died. The beauty of that simplicity is that "me" can be anybody. I am the one sheep, so are you, so is Avery, so is the barista giving you coffee, the murderer in prison, the victim, the newborn, everyone and anyone can be, and is the one sheep. All you have to do is acknowledge that you are lost, and He will find you.

So, Jesus accepted payment for my sin, which is the beginning of the answer as illuminated by Romans 6:23.

For the wages of sin is death, but the gift of God is eternal life throughlin Jesus Christ our Lord (Romans 6:23, KJV). The after the comma is the mind-blowing part. Not only did he accept my punishment, he then gave me his reward for such an altruistic sacrifice. Many struggle with this question because it is an expression that is illogical and perfect love. As human beings, we are incapable of that perfect love and are clouded by logic. For unexplainable things, we chalk up to natural anomalies or flukes. We can answer the question but can never truly appreciate the gravity or significance of that answer.

Jesus died because he chose to accept your punishment so that you may live forever free of any punishment.

I should end it there, but that is my Christian answer. Avery took something else from it that is worth sharing.

Avery: So, he died for me, my sin, even though I don't believe in him?

Me: Yes.

Avery: What if he wasn't the son of God? What if his death was for nothing?

Me: Well, I know that He is, not was, the son of God, but for analytical purposes, I shall play along. More hospitals and schools have been built in the name of Christ than anybody else.

Avery: And more people have died in the name of God.

Me: Absolutely; both Allies and Axis believed God was on their side, and the complicated answer is that He was; we view humanity through a human lens of finite wisdom and linear time.

Avery: Of course we do, but you can't say that God was on the Nazis' side.

Me: There are no sides; he loves all of His children, broken, misdirected, dangerous rabid, lost, ignorant sheep.

Avery: Nazis?

Me: After a mass tragedy, a lone gunman who takes human life in an inexplicable and senseless act of cowardice and evil, what do you do?

Avery: What?

Me: After a mass shooting, what do you do?

Avery: I kiss my kid(s).

Me: Me too, you know why?

Avery: I refuse even to say why.

Me: Me too, but I do one more thing.

Avery: I know. Pray for the families. That does not make you better than me. I think about them. I just don't plead with a mystical invisible man who I think could have stopped it but refused to do the heavy lifting.

Me: Oh, we will be coming back to that…but no, I am not better than you, and yes, I do pray for the victims and their families.

Avery: And you are such an enlightened Christian that you pray for the gunman?

Me: I should, I have, but... not whom I was thinking of...I pray for the gunman's parents. I know sometimes they are abusive; sometimes they are absentee or mentally ill, or whatever, but that is always their baby who will, for the rest of their lives, be a pariah and no longer their beautiful baby...I pray for them.

Avery: OK.

Me: That is how I imagine God feels about all of us, Nazis included.

Avery: I am glad you aren't defending Nazis.

Me: Not at all; Nazis are the historical litmus test for terrible.

Avery: You are saying that your faith, the belief that Jesus died for even Nazis, allows you to see us all as pathetic lost sheep needing a shepherd?

Me: Yup.

Avery: And you find peace in that?

Me: I sure do.

Avery: So, if I am getting this right, Jesus died because he wanted to, and he wanted to because he knew we all deserved to suffer, so he chose to suffer on our behalf, and in doing so, he tripped the system as an undeserving victim thereby giving everyone eternal life.

Me: Yeah, that's it.

Avery: So, your theory, or the theory of Christianity, is that Jesus was ultimately just an awesome guy?

Me: I couldn't say it any better; in fact, that's pretty much the best Biblical footnote ever.

HOW CAN WE HAVE FAITH?

1. *I stopped praying years ago until you told me not to pray; just talk to Him. When I realized I could do that, He felt more real, and my faith was restored.*

2. *I always had faith, it is how I was raised, but it was like a birthmark; it was just a part of me that people could see, but at times I was ashamed of it. I now wear it because I choose to, proudly.*

3. *How can I believe in a benevolent God when I live in a malevolent world?*

4. *I never wanted to be a religious person; it seemed lazy and unintelligent…now I can't start my day without thanking God.*

5. *Having faith means it's a thing you can lose. I thought I lost mine until I found myself being pissed at God… and I can't be pissed at someone I don't believe in. You can lose your faith, but most of us just stuff it in a junk drawer and misuse or neglect it.*

Those are direct quotes from people from ALPHA, a program I participated in, people who did not consider themselves Christians. Faith is not a Christian ideology; it is not even one of religious implications. We spoke earlier of the dead people papers and digital transfer on the non-physical currency that takes faith. Starting your car takes faith. Going to parent-teacher conferences takes faith. Letting your daughter go out on her first date takes faith. Letting your son take out the daughter of a lawyer takes faith. Falling in love takes faith. Being a parent takes faith. All of us live with faith. Having faith is natural. We put stock in things that we experience. Faith is an inherent part of humanity, so the question "How Can We Have Faith?" is to question what it is to be human.

Dr. King said that "faith is taking the first step even when you don't see the whole staircase." This concept was expounded even deeper in a discussion between Avery, a Rabbi, and me.

Avery: I fail to see how we can believe in the great invisible watchmaker and still be logical.

Rabbi: You admit your failure... good first step.

Avery: You know what I mean.

Me: First, get rid of the whole watchmaker thing...not his style...you are far more convoluted and intricate than a watch.

Avery: I just don't know how you get to that point of blind faith.

Rabbi: All faith is blind… in family, government, or technology. I cannot understand how Wi-Fi works or how things charge wirelessly. I don't believe any politician when they speak. I never expect my grandson to listen to his parents or remember my birthday. Yet, I have faith that my iPad will connect to whatever the cloud is and work. I have faith that our military will protect our country and that my rights are absolute, and that the flag stands for freedom. I have faith that my grandson will grow to be a remarkable young man of love and honor. Why do I have such faith…because I have life.

The third quote is where so many get caught up in the struggle with faith. *How can I believe in a benevolent God when I live in a malevolent world?* When this individual said this to me, I could feel their pain. Yet, the quote itself was not an absence of faith but rather an example of struggling to carry the weight of that faith. First, the world is not malevolent. There is malevolence in the world. Suppose you put water in a glass; that does not make the glass only suitable to hold water. There is bad in the world. Violence, hatred, bigotry, pain, disease, hunger, poverty, addiction… and that is just on my block. The existence of evil does not negate the existence of good.

Avery: I know it's cliché, but the question is still a valid one: why does God allow bad things?

Me: Do you think parents allow their kids to become mass shooters or terrorists?

Avery: Some certainly do, but more importantly, are you implying that your God is an impotent parent?

Me: No... I am explaining that free will exists and that God rectifies these evils and wrongs through love and grace.

Avery: Where is the love and grace in a child dying of cancer or being strapped to a bomb?

Me: This is where my faith gives me an advantage because I accept that when that child passes that they are embraced by a loving Father who gives us the grace to go on.

Avery: That is a cheap answer.

Me: I prefer the *easy explanation.*

Avery: Bad things happen to good people, and that is a major chink in your armor.

Me: The problem with your theory is that you presume that people are good. I accept that all humans on this earth are sinners, and sin is an affront to God. Ergo, bad things happen to sinners, and since death is what sinners deserve, I do not see a chink in the armor.

Avery: So, they've got it coming?

Me: As a father and human being, I can never and will never justify disease, death, and violence on children...but...

Avery: But?

Me: But...I am not God. Bad things happen to some people that I would not qualify as bad, and people that I would qualify as bad seem to be blessed in many ways.

Avery: Exactly...it's not fair.

Me: Wrong...it is the definition of fair because it is balanced. I don't know God's plan or His will...I know His instructions, and I do my best at times to follow them, and when I do that...my life is better than when I don't.

PRAYING WITH AN ATHEIST

One of the oldest and played-out questions of faith is, "Why do bad things happen to good people?" This is not a question of faith. It is not one that questions the existence of God but rather the nature of Him. More importantly, it is a grievance. People who ask this question are complaining about the bad they have experienced. This, in turn, means they self-identify as a "good person," which is incredibly arrogant and shows a great lack of humility. Avery went right where everyone always does...kids, a low blow because only a monster can justify the pain, suffering, and death of a child. I have buried children, children I have lost to cancer, suicide, violence, and accidents. That pain is unshakeable. God is not pain; He is not suffering. He is a healer, a deliverer. So, while I cannot justify the seemingly random deaths of children, I can testify that the families of these children who have faith in God find solace, peace, and comfort in that Faith, and those that do not are often bitter, angry, and filled with pain. Granted, there are always exceptions, but the truth is that people of faith accept that the children are not lost...it is us who are lost, suffering, and in pain.

The fifth quote, *"Having faith means it's a thing you can lose. I thought I lost mine until I found myself being pissed at God...and I can't be pissed at someone I don't believe in. You can lose your faith, but most of us just stuff it in a junk drawer and misuse or neglect it."* That is my quote. I said that to a group of people. A group of people who were grieving. It was that quote that actually kicked off this book because Avery was seated across from me when I said it.

Avery: If you can lose it, is it worth having?

Me: I've lost diamond earrings and car keys.

Avery: Ok...I just mean that, why have faith at all in somebody who pisses you off?

Me: You're married, right?

Avery: Yeah, but...let me try it from another angle...

Me: Go for it.

Avery: Why are you here? At this meeting?

Me: Because I wanted someplace to talk about my loss... someplace where being a downer was acceptable and expected.

Avery: Ok, but why couldn't you turn to your God for that?

Me: I did. I still do...and I brought Him here with me.

So, *How Can We Have Faith*? Faith is nothing more than a strong sense of confidence or trust in something. Faith is grown based on experience. You have faith in money because Starbucks accepted your dead people on green paper and gave you your coffee. You have faith in family, friends, coworkers, technology, etc., all because you have personal experience with them doing what they do with, for, and to you. Your relationship is what grows your faith. So, it is simple: to have Faith in God, one needs to nurture a relationship and build on the experiences of that relationship.

HOW AND WHY DO PEOPLE PRAY?

Before addressing the how we should discuss the why; it is a much bigger topic than one would expect. What is prayer? An invocation. An intercession. A devotion. An orison (that was an SAT word that I could not expunge from my brain). Many would define it as a sincere and earnest hope or wish. Others consider some religious gatherings and services to be exercises of prayer. The good old Oxford says prayer is *a solemn request for help or expression of thanks addressed to God or another deity.* A request for help. Interesting. I suppose if you are out on the open water fishing and you want to ask Neptune or Poseidon for some assistance, you do you. Yet, let us examine this from a monotheistic perspective. You see, logically, God has a master plan, and everything goes according to His plan, so our intercession prayers are a waste of time, yet, we are called to and expected to pray. Why? What is the point of asking for help if God is going to do what God is going to do?

Avery: It's pointless and silly, pure and simple.

Me: That's an aggressive stance.

Avery: Come on, man, God's will controls all, but you are gonna ask him for a new bike in His house on His day off?

Me: A tad oversimplified.

Avery: Really? Is it? People pray for money, health, and love...and when prayers aren't answered, they say, "That's just God's will."

Me: Yes, but that doesn't negate anything.

Avery: It makes it an exercise in futility.

Me: How many letters did you write to Santa Claus?

Avery: So, God is as real as Santa?

Me: Well, considering Saint Nicholas of Myra is buried in the Basilica San Nicola in Italy, and I know Santa Claus lives on Long Island, like, I personally know him...yes... God is just as real...so how many letters did you write?

Avery: A lot.

Me: You asked for impossible things, didn't you?

Avery: They shouldn't be impossible for your God.

Me: Our...Our God..., and they aren't impossible for Him..., but since you are being purposely obtuse, I will confess I asked for a Pteranodon for Christmas one year.

Avery: Guessing you didn't get one?

Me: My parents are amazing. Of course, I did. It was 1988, I think, and I got the Pteranodon and every other Dino Rider...but...it wasn't what I asked for: "a real baby Pteranodon."

Avery: And so, you stopped believing in Santa.

Me: No...my mother explained that a real dinosaur could hurt itself or me...I was heartbroken...but...I acknowledged that she was right.

Avery: So, God ignores prayers for healing and help because it is what is best for us?

Me: Yes.

Avery: A mother at the bedside of her dying child pleading for healing, how is that not in her or the child's best interests...your God thinks a kid dying of cancer is a better alternative.

Me: Still our God...and I've personally felt this, and you know that...

Avery: Hence, why I am curious how you can justify *that* prayer being ignored.

Me: Not ignored, just not answered in the way we wanted... God taking a child into His arms rather than healing the child seems cruel to us...because we are selfish beings. Yet, in His perfect love outside of time, He has rescued the child from suffering and pain. He has removed fear, doubt, and the unknown.

Avery: And that seems fair to you, *that* seems right to you?

Me: Not at all...it is infuriating and causes me to be angry with God and filled with bitterness, so how blessed are we that I am not God?

Avery: What?

Me: God makes the decisions we cannot...the fact is that praying for something is not necessarily submitting a request...at least not in my opinion.

Avery: Then why ask?

Me: Because sometimes, we need to let our Dad know what we want even if we know what we want is not what we need...sometimes, it is just about talking to our Dad.

Why we pray is both personal and corporate. Corporately people pray together to give thanks and praise. Personally, people pray for a myriad of reasons...all of which, at their core, are a necessity. Every culture has some sort of exercise of prayer. Eastern Orthodox Hesychasm calls for believers to ritualistically chant the name of Jesus in repetition. Some forms of Buddhism, especially Japanese "Pure Land" Buddhists, have a similar practice of chanting Amida Buddha for sometimes days. Hindu traditions call for fruit sacrifices along with the use of lanterns and incense. The renowned practice of salah for Muslims calls for ritualistic prayer in Arabic five times daily. The use of Tefillin for Jews is a set of small black boxes with verses from the Torah placed in them and strapped to believers' foreheads during prayer. Shinto believers use coins and bells to attract the attention of Kami in order to pass along their requests.

Ritualistic prayer throughout the world exists. It spans socio-economic statuses, races, and faiths. People pray. Sure, not everyone practices the art of, ummm, *baby throwing* that is exercised in the Grishneshwar Temple of Maharashtra, where Muslims and Hindu followers throw babies less than two years of age from a 50-foot tower to men positioned on the ground level with sheets to catch them. Cannibalistic practices of the Aghori are believed by some scholars to be ritualistic prayer, while others believe it is a cultural anomaly related to their faith.

One of the more well-known forms of corporate prayer is the "Minyan Prayer." This is where at least ten orthodox Jews pray together in a room. The prayer is rooted in the connectivity of the believers. Rather than simply reading scripture, they speak with one another and reflect on what they need. It is internal networking. Jobs are found, apartments, houses, dates are set up, teachers are hired, etc. They are rooted in community. They gather together and give thanks to God that they have one another so that together they can be whole in service to God. At Mount Athos, you will find Greek Orthodox men who "pray without ceasing" This is done by the monks who believe that every breath should be in service to Christ as they beseech Him for grace and forgiveness; if they walk, they thank God for the journey, if they shower they thank God for the cleansing power of His grace, if they watch TV they bear witness to the suffering of the world on the news and pray for peace, all actions of every day are an opportunity to pray. Of course, there is the story of Brother Lawrence in prayer, who practiced enjoying the presence of God as he cleaned dishes and prepared meals; his discipline is recounted in a book that will far surpass this one, as it has not been out of print in over three centuries. Catholics have the Rosary, which is a structured repetition of prayers that can be done in groups or individually. Pope Francis has described "The

Five Finger Prayer," in which he explains that the thumb is closest to you, so start by praying for those closest to you. Then comes the index finger, which represents those who guide and teach us. The middle finger is the highest, so we then pray for leaders and those in authority. The ring finger is our weakest digit, so we then pray for the sick and oppressed. Finally, the pinky, the smallest finger, reminds us to humbly pray for ourselves... a pretty *handy* prayer if you ask me...eh...eh? Anyway, there are times when we do not have words to pray for what we feel. In some cultures and faiths, this will bring about different rituals and, at times, will result in the gift of speaking in tongues. However, Quakers have another practice of prayer where congregants will meet weekly and sit in silence for a prayer meeting that many call "Holding In The Light." Here, believers gather together to sit in the light of God's grace and impart, "God, I have no words; help me see as you see, love as you love, and please do the work that only you can." Corporate pleas to God are not always Religious specific. In Israel, at the Western Wall, Christians, Jews, and Muslims all exercise their faith together in beseeching God for peace. Prayer unifies and connects people not only to God but to one another.

Corporate prayer connects believers, and those believers connect to God; personal prayer is just as important, yet, much harder to describe the "how." Every faith has its prayers. New believers, questioning believers, and even "seasoned" believers all struggle with how to pray. Understandably, many of us have heard the term "put the fear of God into" or have heard someone described as a "good Godfearing person." Then you are expected to go and talk to this all-imposing Fear Monger. Hard pass. Yet, if we strip away "the law" of religion and break down the personal interest of prayer, it can be beautiful. Shake away Fear and replace it with Reverence. Do not expect punishment, but long for righteousness. You will see the perception shift from Intimidating to Loving.

In my personal experience, I was raised with formal and ritualistic prayers. There were prayers that I memorized and recited on command. Prayers that have meaning and, if understood, believed, and meant, are inspirational and awe-inspiring. However, I will be honest, the majority of them were just memorized, and I didn't take the time to dissect and appreciate them; I just repeated them when I needed to in accordance with my religious instruction. So, imagine my surprise when I grew in my faith and understood Matthew 6:7 NIV, which says *and when you pray, do not keep on babbling like pagans, for they think they will be heard because of their many words.* I was babbling most of my prayer life, just saying words, and here it is, words in *red* telling me explicitly not to do that, just two verses from a prayer that I had committed to memory and verbally regurgitated more times than I can count. So, I was lost. I had no idea how to pray. Had.

At my Church, they have "Beholding Sets," which are small group gatherings in which we sit in praise of Christ. No agenda, just worship. This is where I learned how to pray, and since you've made it this far, I might as well share. First off, you need to understand something. I do not specifically enjoy sitting in worship sets. Some of the songs annoy me because of their repetition. Then there are the other congregants; some speak in tongues, not a gift I have or am I particularly fond of as it is sometimes loud and unexpectedly scares the life out of me. Other members will start randomly running around, crying, yelling, dancing, singing the wrong lyrics, and clapping completely off-beat. It drives me absolutely insane. You see, I have a very structured brain. The structure may not make sense to many...but it makes sense to me. So, these "distractions" can be devastating to my mental stability at times as they are all I can focus on to the point where my eye starts twitching and I am filled with a rage equal to the fire intensity of a hundred super nova stars because this reverent and beautiful exercise of worship appears to my head to be a chaotic cavalcade of havoc and bedlam. So, one night as this perfect storm was brewing, I tried to block it all out and literally just started talking to Jesus. Conversationally, no candles, no chants, no ritual, just conversationally. Now, the issue with conversationally talking to Jesus out loud is that you appear to be mad. So, in the aforementioned worship setting, I was fine. Yet, I fell asleep. It was at night; it was a long day, and my brain was working overtime. As I slept, I met Jesus at a lakeside, drank some sweet tea, and had a chat. Best. Prayer. Ever. Granted, I have ridiculed and mocked people who have claimed to "speak to God." Here I stand, in all my hypocritical glory, doing the same thing. Truth is what it is.

That's my story. Now, before you throw the book or call for me to be burned at the stake, hear me out. I am in no way claiming to be a prophet or any wise anything. I am saying that is how prayer worked for me. That is how I was able to plug into my faith, with conversation and reverent familiarity. You see, Christianity is regularly viewed as teaching that Jesus died for all our sins. The truth is, He died for me. Just me and just you; it really is that personal. If the rest of you "Saints" were free from all sin and debauchery (I have TV and internet service, so, off the high horse) and Jesus knew that just me, my lowly sinner self, would exist in the future, He still goes to the cross. It seems like the sort of thing you should say "thank you" for...so start there. Yet, maybe you aren't even ready to start there. Maybe that is still too much. Start with questioning. "God, are you really there?" is, in my opinion, a fine starting point for prayer. Don't demand proof. The Creator of all existence need not prove Himself to you; it is quite the opposite. However, ask your questions, share your doubts, and ask about the pain and suffering of the world. Just talk. Prayer is the chance to talk, not so that He hears, because He already knows what you are going to say. Talk so you hear it. Talk so you acknowledge your doubts, fears, anger, joys, and gratitude. You owe it not only to God but to yourself to open up and talk it out. Therapy works because you get to open up safely. I love my kids, and I assure them that they can tell me anything. I support, nurture and provide for them. I am not a perfect man, and I struggle with being called a "good man"; however, I love my children and pride myself on being a father. Matthew 7:11 NIV says *if you, then, though you are evil, know how to give good gifts to your children, how much more will your Father in heaven give good gifts to those who ask him.* That verse, right there, is the root of prayer. Ask Him!

THE BIBLE, HOW
AND WHY SHOULD
WE READ IT

A book so popular that the NY Times removed it from consideration in determining "Best Sellers" as it would be unfair. No other publication comes close to record sales. No book has been translated into more languages, recorded, revered, disputed, and discussed. When it was originally comprised, it was written in three languages. Most of The Old Testament was in Hebrew. Of course, there were Ezra and Daniel, who just had to be different, as they were transcribed in Aramaic, and the New Testament was written in Greek. Easy to see why there are so many "translations." The original language provided a Bible with 611,000 words...when translated to English, that number jumps up significantly. In fact, the King James translation has a word count of 788,280. Lots of words, so where to start?

Many say they want to get the largest book of the Bible done with first; that would be the book of Jeremiah.

Unless you have got one of those 15th Century Bibles, then it would be the Book of Kings. Of Course, if you have ancient Manuscripts, it would be the Torah, which is the culmination of Genesis, Exodus, Leviticus, Numbers, and Deuteronomy. So, length may not be the easiest way to determine how to read the Bible. Yet, if you insist on this method, start with 3 John. You will be done in about a minute and can say you have started to read the Bible and are already done with a Book.

Of course, you could try and start by author. But good luck with that. It is generally accepted that there are more than 40 authors of the Bible. The beauty of this book is that all these authors weave one message. Kings, farmers, fishermen, prophets, a physician, a scribe, musicians, and priests are just a small cross-section of who these authors are. To date, nobody has a signed copy. Many people credit Moses for writing the Torah, but he was dead during some of the events written about in the first five books. There is a dispute over who wrote Jonah since many believe it was not Jonah, or at the very least editorial content of repentant cows was added after he wrote it. Kings, Esther, Joshua, and Job are not designated to any specific authors but look at the titles; again, some editorials may have been added. Then there is Hebrews; nobody knows who wrote it. Paul, Apollos, and even Barnabas have been given credit. I suppose the Gospels are easy; look at the name. Of course, there is the 2 Peter dispute. Yet, pseudepigraphy is not a topic we must tackle in this simple book. You could tackle Paul and his writing spree to get yourself started.

PRAYING WITH AN ATHEIST

Our commonly used English translations have grouped the books of the Bible based on the nature of the book rather than by chronology or author. For instance, the Old Testament has Law, History, Wisdom, Poetry then Prophets. The TaNaKh, Judaic Hebrew Bible, arranges books differently. The Torah are books of law, followed by Prophets, which blend poetry, history, and prophecies. In this composition, the final book is Chronicles, not Malachi. My point is that a chronological approach is not necessarily the best approach.

Maybe you like music. Well, you are in luck, as there are at least 185 songs in the Bible. I say at least because that is just the portions of Scripture that are identified as "song," "psalm," "dirge," or "chant." Fascinatingly approximately 150 of them are in the book of Psalms. If you want love songs, we have you covered in The Song of Solomon, an epic love song between a bride and bridegroom. Are you a tad emo? Try Lamentations, a set of five dirges mourning the collapse of Jerusalem. Are you a fan of long anthems? Psalm 119 is your jam; at 1,732 words, it is a Bible Study anthem focusing on the significance of God's word. Do you prefer jingles? Get over to 2 Chronicles 5:13 and 20:21. If you know Hebrew, it's only seven words. Do you like to see how an artist changes over time? The Bible is the place to see it. Exodus 15 shows us Moses singing the first song of the Bible as children safely cross the Red Sea. Revelations 15 has John seeing those who have overcome the beast singing "the song of Moses," new lyrics, same victorious spirit. So, if this is your thing, dive in and start singing some of your favorite Biblical tunes in the shower.

Maybe you are more interested in the geographical regions where the Bible was authored. As a history buff, I can appreciate such an approach. However, most of the Bible was written in Israel, while much of Jeremiah was transcribed in Egypt, and several New Testament books were written in European cities, meaning that The Bible spans three continents; considering the age and composition of The Bible, in and of itself is proof positive to many believers that the Bible is divinely inspired even if written by man.

You want dreams; we've got dreams. Six kings, two Josephs, and Pontius Pilate's wife give us twenty-one dreams that span five different books of the Bible. Ten of those twenty-one are in the book of Genesis.

You want to be told what to do; James is for you, lovingly called the bossiest book of the Bible; it contains at least sixty-one imperatives in just one hundred eight verses. So, 2.6% of the words in James are imperative verbs. Great place to start if you want to be charged with not just hearing the Word but also living it. If that's too much, try Joel, same thing, just a little less.

The truth is that there are more researched and eloquent Bible study books that help people navigate the **HOW**. I have always found that first picking the right translation is essential. The spectrum of translation is something that is both studied and debated. The spectrum runs from Literal word-for-word translation to thought-for-thought translation. Here is a handy list of translations from the

most literal to the most functional paraphrased. I am sure
I missed some.

- Interlinear
- New American Standard Bible (NASB)
- Amplified
- English Standard Version (ESV)
- Revised Standard Version (RSV)
- King James Version (KJV)
- New King James Version (NKJV)
- Holman Christian Study Bible (HCSB)
- New Revised Standard Version (NRSV)
- New American Bible (NAB)
- New Jerusalem Bible (NJB)
- New International Version (NIV)
- Today's New International Version (TNIV)
- God's Word Translation (GW)
- New Century Version (NCV)
- International Children's Bible (ICB)
- New Living Translation (NLT)
- Common English Bible (CEB)
- New International Reader's Version (NIRV)
- Good News Translation (GNT)
- Contemporary English Version (CEV)
- The Living Bible
- The Message

Many people have strong opinions about which translation
is "right." Again, nobody has a properly autographed Bible.
Your choice of translation should be reflective of why you
are reading it: literal translation, colloquial language, or a

blend. Once you get into it, you will find yourself bouncing from translation to translation for certain passages and verses for a deeper understanding and appreciation. The point is that **HOW** should be determined by the **WHY**. So, why read the Bible?

First off, it is a great way to unlearn. Reading the Bible is an amazing way to brain-dump misinformation. Find where in the Bible "The Trinity" is mentioned. It does not, this is a doctrine created by Biblical understanding and is supported by teachings, but the Bible does not mention "The Trinity" at any point. Or where in the Bible it states that Mary Magdalene was a prostitute? Nowhere. Pope Gregory I, in 591, combined Mary Magdalene with Mary of Bethany and the Unnamed Woman of Luke 7:36-50 to create a narrative of redemption in his sermons following Easter. Or identify in the book of Genesis, where apples got a bad reputation since the fruit was never identified. The name Lucifer comes from the translation of Isaiah 14:12. At no time is the Serpent of Eden, or Satan, called Lucifer in the Bible; in fact, at no time is the serpent identified as Satan. The whole two by two procession into the Ark, nope, not Biblical. Judaic dietary law identifies animals by cleanliness, clean animals went in groups of seven, and unclean animals went in pairs. There are Ten Commandments, right? Not if you read Exodus. There are fourteen or fifteen statements that certain religions have taken the liberty to combine, some to create the core list of ten that we know so well. The three kings who come to Christ's birth are so renowned that they must be Biblical, well, not so much. In fact, in Scripture, they are not referenced as kings, nor are they identified as traveling in a group of three. The number comes from the three gifts presented. The list goes on and on...so read your Bible if you want to know what the Bible actually says.

Is the Bible still relevant? Aren't there non-Biblical texts that can teach the same thing? The truth is that there are so many texts that will try to explain, elaborate or replace The Bible. However, as so many of us have said after leaving a movie theater...*The Book Was Better.* The reason we should read the Bible is because it is living word. Nations have been formed on its word. Empires have fallen because of its word. Lives have been saved, relationships formed, and countless people have experienced love, compassion, belonging, and understanding from the words found within. When we say it is a living word, what do we mean? 1 John 1:1-4 talks about how Jesus represents the Living Word of God. John tells us that Jesus is God's presence manifested, His promise materialized, and His Word among us. The Word of God is both the literal word and a manifestation of His presence. At this juncture, the language becomes flowery and convoluted, making people believe we are talking in code because we are clueless. So, let me simplify it.

WHY READ THE BIBLE? Because it works. There is a reason it has never been out of circulation. There is a reason it is the most translated literary work in the history of humanity. It literally speaks to the human condition.

A woman was sexually assaulted at a party. She went to the police but could not identify the assailant as she was intoxicated. Her friend gave her a Bible and said, "Find refuge here." The woman threw the Bible in frustration and told her friend to leave. After throwing her friend out, she started to cry and screamed that she would rather be dead. She went to wash her face and stepped on the Bible she had tossed. It was opened to Deuteronomy 22:25-26 NIV. Only *the man who has done this shall die. Do nothing to the woman; she has committed no sin deserving death.*

A man returned home from Vietnam and was greeted by an old friend as his family disowned him because they protested the war. He was crippled by depression and anxiety and was later diagnosed with PTSD. He spent years in therapy, was medicated, and after serving his country, he was on the street filled with despair. He lived believing he was a villain, called himself a monster, a killer, and was terrified at what would become of him. When asked how to describe his day in group therapy, he would always respond, "discouraged." He met a Pastor at a soup kitchen several years later who handed him a random paper bag with some snacks, mittens, a hat, a book, a puzzle, some toiletries, and small scrap of paper which read, *Have I not commanded you? Be strong and courageous. Do not be terrified; do not be discouraged, for the Lord your God will be with you wherever you go* – Joshua 1:9 ESV. The man is now married, has two children and a granddaughter, and is a grief counselor.

These are two simple testimonies of the power of The Word. William J. Toms is credited with saying, "Be careful how you live. You may be the only Bible some person ever reads."

This quote is generally used to help inspire people to live more Christlike. However, in the context of The Bible itself, it speaks volumes. It exemplifies the nature of the Living Word because it affects people globally. No matter where you are or aren't in your walk of faith, The Bible holds the answers. It can and will inspire, move, heal, and change you...if you let it,

Avery: If I don't believe in God, why would I read the Bible?

Me: Why wouldn't you?

Avery: I see you're giving up discussion and opting for why not arguments.

Me: Not at all. I'm just curious why a non-believer would take issue with reading it.

Avery: Because there is no point.

Me: You've read post-apocalyptic fiction and books about prepubescent magicians...but stories of redemption, miracles, unity, and triumph offend you?

Avery: It's different.

Me: How so?

Avery: I'm not interested in stories of people being dammed to the fiery pits of hell to be tormented because they didn't follow your rules.

Me: Ok...then don't read Dante's "Divine Comedy."

Avery: What?

Me: The rings of hell are from Dante, not the Bible

Avery: ...

So, **HOW** to read the Bible is a matter of personal preference. I suggest, top of the page, left to right...if it is an English translation. **WHY** to read the Bible is because you owe it to yourself to see how for thousands of years, a book has brought millions of people to peace and salvation... basically...Why Not?

DOES GOD REALLY GUIDE ANYBODY?

Avery: God has a divine plan, right?

Me: Yes.

Avery: And everything fits into His plan?

Me: I suppose.

Avery: Nazis, earthquakes, famine, disease...all part of His plan?

Me: Look, I'm not God or His PR Rep...but that's not how I see it.

Avery: But that's the part that gets me. You can't say it is all part of His grand plan and then brush off the negative stuff.

Me: Not brushing it off...you ski, right?

Avery: Yeah, do you?

Me: Absolutely not.

Avery: OK then.

Me: You drive to Vermont or Pennsylvania or wherever to ski

Avery: Yeah, got a place in Vermont.

Me: So, assuming you and the family plan a trip to Vermont and along the way, some drunk driver smashes into a truck which hits the guardrail and shuts down the highway for three exits...do you not go?

Avery: No...but...

Me: Hold your but... you plan to go skiing in Vermont. A detour, tragic or otherwise, would not alter your plan to gracefully fall down a hill with comically large shoes on... but you think that the Divine Creator of the cosmos could not adapt to detours of any kind for His plan to save all of humanity?

Before answering the question honestly, we must understand what is being asked. Does God really guide anybody? Guidance is a relatively subjective concept. A guide dog will literally drag a person around to get them to where they need to be, the owner could pull the dog, but ultimately the dog directs. Navigation apps are a tad less controlling, as they tell you how to get there, and as you inevitably miss your exit, they will reroute and continue to suggest your path. Then there are trains, or more appropriate, considering how our lives are...rollercoasters; you strap in, and they bring you, and so long as all goes well, you don't get derailed. So, what sort of *guidance* do we normally associate with God?

God's Grand Design is a concept many people get stuck on. Well, have no fear. After centuries of conflict, confusion, debate, and wars, I have the answer. What is God's Grand

Design? What is His plan? None of your business or concern. That's the answer, stop obsessing over it because, for a species of beings that have a hard time building a bookshelf from IKEA, I do not think we are equipped to comprehend the infinite knowledge and plan of the Creator of the cosmos. However, such a faith-based answer seems to be a copout, so I proffer that we do not worry about God's plan and instead focus on our part in it. Which begs the question, what is our role?

Try. Cats on branches with the saying "Just hang in there" adorn offices across the country. Since I was a child, I loathed them. Do not just hang in there. Try, pull yourself up, and make an effort to do better, to be better. That is our role. We will fail. We define ourselves on our ability to fail (it is human to err, I'm only human, etc.); in the deep recesses of our minds, we accept failure. That is a good thing, to a degree, because it means we shouldn't be crippled by it. A failure is just another chance to succeed. We all know the cliches of *it is how many times you get back up.* Henry Ford once said, "Failure is only the opportunity to begin again, this time more intelligently." There is no shortage of quotes and adages to help lift the spirit when needed. Yet, my personal favorite is Philippians 1:6 NIV, which states, *being confident of this, that he who began a good work in you will carry it on to completion until the day of Jesus Christ.*

The Apostle Paul was undoubtedly a major force in the formation of the early Church and a cornerstone of what is known as "Christianity." For me, that first chapter and sixth verse of his letter to the Philippians is the ultimate "hang in there" quote, and I opine would make a much better poster than that poor cat clinging for life. I believe this scripture is the epitome of uplifting quotes because it is not just about doing good and moving forward; it is a reminder that you are doing good work. It is a message of hope that tells the reader they are not alone. A surgeon who successfully completes a heart transplant will take more pride in his child's first soccer goal because we pour so much of our purpose into our children's lives. So, if we, as pathetic mortals, are that way, how greater is the pride of God? You will succeed, get back up, and do better because you will never have to do it alone. If you walk toward Christ and follow God's path before you, all will be fine.

Yet, what does all this inspirational mumbo jumbo have to do with the question at hand? Does God guide us? If so...how?

The concept of conscience spans millennia, religions, and cultures. The Ancient Greeks had philosophical debates on the morality of man. They determined that the propensity for evil was only kept in check by internal control, known as *suneidesis* or, in Latin, *conscientia*, the root of both "conscience" and "consciousness." *Conscience* is defined as an inner feeling or voice viewed as acting as a guide to the rightness or wrongness of one's behavior. That is not my definition. That is Oxford Dictionary's definition—a VOICE acting to GUIDE. *Consciousness* is defined as the state of being awake or aware of one's surroundings.

Avery: Right and wrong are not uniquely Christian.

Me: Not at all.

Avery: Christians are just as capable of evil as non-believers.

Me: Well...that ultimately depends on how you define Christianity.

Avery: Anybody who believes in God and Jesus.

Me: Oh,...then, absolutely.

Avery: Shouldn't God protect his believers and make sure they don't go astray?

Me: Yeah.

Avery: So, are you saying Christians aren't just as misguided as everyone else?

Me: Working with your definition, no, because belief in something is not enough. Faith requires more of a commitment. You have parents...do they love you?

Avery: Yes.

Me: Would you agree that they want to protect and guide you?

Avery: It's different.

Me: Just answer the question.

Avery: Of course.

Me: Did you always listen to them?

Avery: No.

Me: Are your poor choices the fault of your parents?

Avery: No, but my parents aren't magical omnipotent beings who could've stopped my bad choices.

Me: How lucky for you...but...there's our difference.

Avery: What?

Me: For starters, for me, Christianity is more than a belief. It is a relationship of love and obedience; knowing of someone and having a relationship with someone is vastly different, and my understanding of God's omnipotence is just as much His ability not to act and control our actions as it is His ability to do so.

Avery: So, being absentee makes Him a better God?

Me: Far from absentee, I see God as the first parent to realize that "helicopter parenting" does not work...so, He gives us the freedom and ability to do what we want and waits patiently for us to realize He is not only right, but He is there for us, no matter what.

Proverbs 16:9 NLT clearly states, *"We can make our plans, but the Lord determines our steps."* How do we reconcile this with the concept of free will? This sounds more like control than guidance. King Solomon is credited as the author of Proverbs, and "determines" may not be the best translation. Some translations say *A man's heart devised his way, but the LORD directed his steps.* (NKJV)

Free will is real. No matter what your faith is. People make choices. Christianity is not opposed to this ideal. We do as we want; that is what makes us human (see Job 23:13). We must own our choices because they are birthed from our desires and thoughts (see 1 Corinthians 2:11), whether we be guided by constant logical planning (see James 4:13) or the desires of our hearts (see Proverbs 4:23) we decide.

In Scripture, "the heart" is akin to desires, wants, and emotions...not evil, but susceptible. Again, not a distinctly Christian outlook. When guided by desire, we can be easily led astray by substance abuse, violence, infidelity, immorality, etc. Just because it is what makes us "feel good" at the moment does not make it "good" for us (see Jeremiah 17:9). Yet, we so often justify our desires. I have heard countless spouses blame the "unavailability" of their partner as the reason they strayed in their marriage. I have also heard addicts state that the substances kept them from deeper and darker problems. While these instances may have grains of truth, the fact remains that our choices are ours, and we make excuses to justify our wrongs. I'll stop sugarcoating it; let us call it what it is...SIN. We will always find a way to justify our sins (see Proverbs 27:19).

So, *We Make Our Plans.* That is evident. We can easily break our choices down like a balance sheet adorned with debits and credits, pluses and minuses, ebbs and flows, etc. However, to do so ignores the sovereignty of God. That inner voice, the Conscience, let's name it, Hayden Smith, another nice gender-neutral name. So, Hayden advises us of what is right and wrong, but where does that definition come from? Hayden does not introduce this concept of morality; he reminds us of it. If SIN is the attractive choice, the desire, why are we so conflicted with the "good" choices? For me, the explanation is easy; wrong is against our original coding, and the original code was written in Genesis 1:26. After that, it was corrupted, and a virus, SIN, changed our original code and brought in choice. Right is our default, and Hayden is like that annoying old-school paperclip that used to pop up in Windows programs to help guide you. The truth is that all too often, we quickly "x" out Hayden, but that does not stop the advice from coming.

But The Lord Determines Our Steps. We think as mortals. As an American, my mindset is based on American History, which is minor compared to Imperialistic Western Society, which western Society is almost insignificant in comparison to Civilized Society, which Civilized Society is dwarfed in comparison to Human History; and according to many trains of thought, Human History is but a drop in the bucket of time here on earth, let alone the universe. The Creator of the universe probably has a vastly different watch on His wrist than we do. So, while we plan, scheme, and plot our lives, as chaos reigns around us, we are guided by the universal truth of Isiah 46:10, His will prevails. His determination of our steps is not in opposition to our will but in spite of it. If our hearts push us toward sin, He weighs in and whispers to our hearts (see Proverbs 21:2). God sets the destination; Hayden provides turn-by-turn directions (see Jeremiah 10:23). If our plan does not lineup with the will of God, it doesn't pan out, God controls all of creation. Your wanting to join the circus may not factor into that. (see Psalm 135:6). We plan, and God laughs, is a concept that permeates even non-believers. Yet, there is an air of truth to it because the idea of "fate" or "destiny" is not a distinctly Christian ideal;

PRAYING WITH AN ATHEIST

in fact, many Christians clutch their pearls when hearing such words because we often focus on the connotation and societal use of a word, rather than the definition. However, as a Christian, I have accepted that no human on earth can escape the path God has set for them (see Daniel 4:35), and rather than feeling like a prisoner of that, I take comfort in the fact that I have a purpose and am excited by seeing it unfold and come to fruition. My worth is seen despite my best efforts to mess it up with my consistent choice of sin.

You're ten years old. You wake up Saturday morning at 8 am. You plan to watch cartoons, play a video game, eat all the marshmallows out of the cereal, and play outside with your friends. The clock strikes 10 am, and your dad tells you to get dressed because you are visiting your Great Aunt at the nursing home. What we plan is not always what happens. In our lives, sometimes what is done is decided for us…and sometimes it is decided *FOR* us.

I suppose the best way to answer the meaning of Proverbs 16:9 is to refer to Proverbs 19:21 NIV; *"Many are the plans in a person's heart, but it is the LORD's purpose that prevails."*

No matter your plans, your choices, your will, right, wrong, or indifferent (which isn't really a thing), the fact remains that the Will of God remains steadfast. We often doubt ourselves. We question our choices and seek wisdom and advice. The best advice we usually receive is from Hayden Smith, that little voice inside of us. Trust that voice; it is there for a reason.

Romans 8:28 tells us that God will work through ALL THINGS for the good of those who love Him and have been called according to His purpose. That is good news. No matter what our choices, decisions, missteps, and actions are that God will work through them for good, for His will, His plan for us, for the best of us and the best for us. The great news is that all of us have been called. The better news is that we were built to love Him. So, in short, He's got your back.

So, does God guide us? Short answer...yes.

MEET HAYDEN SMITH

Hayden Smith, the arbitrary and gender-neutral name assigned in our last chapter to that little voice that directs us away from sin. That feeling we get when we are guided to love and wholesomeness. That unexpected warmth we feel when embraced with love and compassion.

Hayden Smith is a person, indeed not known by that name, but we had to come up with some name to get through that chapter to explain the fact that this voice, this guidance, this counselor, helper, protector, this was not just a part of our psyche, as it exists separate from us and that is why we turn to it. Hayden is not some indescribable "force." It is a real person. A friend you can call upon whenever you are in need.

Now is the point where my Pastor, my cousin, my aunt, and countless others get annoyed because of my lack of reverence. Hayden Smith is nothing more than a literary moniker for "Holy Spirit,"…and not a very creative one at that. I used this "name" to point out the relationship that we all have with The Holy Spirit before identifying that it was Him whom we interact with. It is a sad truth that many are more comfortable with crystal balls, mediums, tarot cards, and Jiminy Cricket than they are with the religiosity of the Holy Spirit. Hayden Smith, your conscience, the sense of righteousness…all of that was the Holy Spirit the whole time, and I just Scooby Doo'd this whole thing. So…

WHO IS THE HOLY SPIRIT?

The concept of the Holy Spirit is one that confuses even the most devout Christians. The truth is that, like all my proffered answers, mine are based on my experiences and faith. As I have done with Avery and countless others, I invite you to have discussions with friends, family, confidants, and teachers. The Holy Spirit is not some mystical force; the Holy Spirit is a person, a divine person with an individual mind and will. Scripture simply defines the Holy Spirit as "God."

Acts 5:3-4 shows us Peter confronting Ananias because he lied to the Holy Spirit, and he tells him in no uncertain terms that he had lied not to men but to *God Himself.* This statement identifies that lying to the Holy Spirit is lying to God.

Psalm 139:7 tells us that the Holy Spirit has the omnipresent characteristic of God. A characteristic that is only expounded upon by Paul in his letters to the Corinthians when he writes in 1 Corinthians 2:10-11 NIV; *these are the things God has revealed to us by His Spirit. The Spirit searches all things, even the deep things of God. For who knows a person's thoughts except for their own spirit within them? In the same way, no one knows the thoughts of God except the Spirit of God.* So, while the Holy Spirit is God, He is also clearly identifiable as separate from God.

The Holy Spirit is indubitably a distinct and individual person, divine and real.

As a person, He thinks and knows, as again stated in 1 Corinthians 2:10 NIV; *these are the things God has revealed to us by His Spirit. The Spirit searches all things, even the deep things of God.*

Ephesians 4:30 NIV shows us that He can be wronged; *[a]nd do not grieve the Holy Spirit of God, with whom you were sealed for the day of redemption.*

He works on our behalf and for our well-being as He intercedes to God as written in Romans 8:26-27 NIV; *In the same way, the Spirit helps us in our weakness. We do not know what we ought to pray for, but the Spirit himself intercedes for us through wordless groans. And he who searches our hearts knows the mind of the Spirit because the Spirit intercedes for God's people in accordance with the will of God.*

He acts in accordance with the will of God as again stated by Paul in 1 Corinthians 12:7-11 NIV; *Now to each one the manifestation of the Spirit is given for the common good. To one there is given through the Spirit a message of wisdom, to another a message of knowledge by means of the same Spirit, to another faith by the same Spirit, to another gift of healing by that one Spirit, to another miraculous powers, to another prophecy, to another distinguishing between spirits, to another speaking in different kinds of tongues and to still another the interpretation of tongues. All these are the work of one and the same Spirit, and he distributes them to each one, just as he determines.*

So, Scripture can surely back up the reality and individual existence of The Holy Spirit. Jesus promised us this Comforter and Counselor, and it is in The Holy Spirit that we find it. I have always found it odd that Pentecost is not as widely celebrated and revered as Easter. It is the celebration and recognition of Jesus' promise to us in the reception of The Holy Spirit (see John 14:16, 26, 15:26)...but NO, let us all hide eggs and eat chocolate rabbits, but I digress.

Avery: Honestly, it's the whole Trinity thing that confuses me.

Me: Why?

Avery: Because a person cannot be multiple people.

Me: Well...I find that limiting God to the constraints of humanity is a terrible idea, but let's run with that.

Avery: How?

Me: Well, Batman, Superman, Ironman, they are all both human and hero.

Avery: And fictitious...so I guess we are done?

Me: (laughs) OK…fair shot…what about you?

Avery: I am no hero.

Me: What about to your kids? You are a parent. You are an employee. You are a friend. You are a child. You are a cousin. You are a spouse. You are a teacher. You are a student…

Avery: OK, OK. Those are just roles.

Me: Maybe to you…but not to your kids, your spouse, or your parents. It is not a role; it is a definition of who you are based on your relationship.

Avery: OK

Me: OK?...that's it?

Avery: I don't see the point. I wear many hats. Who doesn't?

Me: Again, not about role, about relationship…to your kid, you are not and will never be a spouse. That is not a role to them…You are a Parent…period…not a role, an identity based on a relationship.

Avery: Uh huh

Me: And if a pathetic skin sack of bones like you can be all of that, how can you deny that God can be three…just three

Avery: Pathetic…Skin…Sack…of Bones

Me: Too much?

WHAT DOES THE HOLY SPIRIT DO?

Counsels. That is the short answer.

Yet, a Man far wiser than I told us exactly what The Holy Spirit does. In John 14:26 NIV, Jesus tells us, *"The Holy Spirit, whom the Father will send in my name, he will teach you all things and bring to your remembrance all that I have said to you."* When society falls, it is said that Soldiers, Farmers, Doctors, and Lawyers will be needed. Soldiers to keep the peace, Farmers to keep the food, Doctors to keep the health, and Lawyers to keep them in check. Many would argue that list, but I use it to highlight the fact that The Holy Spirit is our Counselor. The Greek word is *Parakletos*, which some translations equate to "Helper," and in others, it is "Counselor," and in translation, the same meaning as "Legal Counsel." The position of an individual who petitions the Judge for the life of another. That is what The Holy Spirit does, counsels those who will listen. Jesus knew He was ascending, and so He gave us an advocate and teacher.

What do counselors do? In addition to guiding and teaching, they convict. Prosecutors collect and provide evidence to convict wrongdoers in society. The Holy Spirit does this as well. By highlighting sin, the Holy Spirit ushers in a righteous judgment for the world. In John 16:7-8 NIV, again Jesus advises us *very truly, I tell you, it is for your good that I am going away. Unless I go away, the Advocate will not come to you; but if I go, I will send him to you. When he comes, he will prove the world to be in the wrong about sin and righteousness, and judgment.* You know when you've done wrong. That sense of guilt is not to punish us; it is intended to correct us. We don't tell children not to do certain things because we are boring and lame; we do so for their safety.

Our love for them has us try and steer them toward making the right choices. That is what the Holy Spirit does. When you hide that text from your spouse. When you take that extra drink. When you look at that website you shouldn't open. Whatever it may be, that guilt, that shame, that is love, that is guidance, that is convicting wrong within you. That is what The Holy Spirit does.

Another role of The Holy Spirit is to be a permanent tenant on rent control, with their lifetime rent being paid in full. Paul writes in 1 Corinthians 3:16 NIV, *"Don't you know that you yourselves are God's temple and that God's Spirit dwells in your midst?"* The Holy Spirit resides within us. Even the Oxford Dictionary admitted that your conscience is an "inner voice"...that is a voice that resides within you, guiding you and teaching you right from wrong. This takes me back to my Pentecost point. You are a temple of God, with The Spirit of God, that same Spirit that floated above creation in the Book of Genesis, That Holy Spirit as promised by Jesus, that Spirit resides in you. If you're honest with yourself, you know it to be true. There are moments when you know exactly what to do or say when that knowledge is beyond you. There are moments when you are on the wrong path, and internally you are turned away from sin and guided toward something far greater than yourself. Everyday miracles happen inside you regularly. You may call it coincidence, chance, luck, or conscience, yet, you know it is more than your natural being. You know that there is something supernatural that happens within you, and it protects and guides you. You know your tenant, so it is time to start cultivating a positive relationship with The Holy Spirit.

Another task of The Holy Spirit is to provide us with knowledge and strength. God has given us This Counselor so that we may be drawn closer to Him. The Holy Spirit allows us to know God better since He is, in fact, the spirit of God. As God's Spirit, He knows the thoughts of God and will reveal them to those who trust and believe in Him. In fact, it is the Holy Spirit that believers encounter, that is, who gives rise to faith. Our first real connection with God or even Christ is through The Holy Spirit because He is who is here, with us, always. The Holy Spirit opens our eyes and minds to salvation and grace. Jesus knew that his disciples and all who would follow would need the power to carry out their work. In Act 1:8 NIV, Jesus tells His disciples, "You *will receive power when the Holy Spirit comes on you, and you will be my witnesses in Jerusalem, and in all Judea and Samaria, and to the ends of the earth.*" The Ends Of The Earth...that's you, that's me...that is us. That power resides within us. It resides in the surgeon saving a child, a mother giving birth, a teacher reaching a neglected child, and a woman loving a broken man. That is the awesome power of The Holy Spirit that resides within us. All of us have access to this power and wisdom. Paul wrote to the Ephesians, "*I keep asking that the God of our Lord Jesus Christ, the glorious Father, may give you the Spirit of wisdom and revelation, so that you may know him better. I pray that the eyes of your heart may be enlightened in order that you may know the hope to which he has called you, the riches of his glorious inheritance in his holy people and his incomparably great power for us who believe. That power is the same as the mighty strength he exerted when he raised Christ from the dead and seated him at his right hand in the heavenly realms"* (Ephesians 1:17-20 NIV).

In John 16:13 ESV, the Holy Spirit is called the "Spirit of Truth." This is because He guides all who believe in absolute truth, God's truth. The Holy Spirit only speaks what He knows, and as The Spirit of God, all He knows is truth and glory. Again, that is INSIDE YOU.

Another thing that The Holy Spirit does is dole out gifts. These gifts are both controversial and well-documented. Paul went through the trouble of writing them down, in no particular order, in 1 Corinthians 12:7-11. Rather than delve into them, let us rationalize this. There are people who are smarter, more gifted, etc. Why? Many receive the same education and have similar backgrounds and statuses; however, we all have different strengths, and at certain times in our lives, these strengths are regularly used to help others in a way that would and should glorify God himself. That is the doing of the Holy Spirit. You have a gift, I have no idea what it is, but I assure you that you have one, and you have it because The Holy Spirit has given it to you so that you may glorify God. The beauty in glorifying God is that it makes the world a better place, makes you happier and healthier, and all around improves everything.

Another role of The Holy Spirit is to brand all believers. Paul writes in Ephesians 1:13 NIV, *"[a]nd you also were included in Christ when you heard the message of truth, the gospel of your salvation. When you believed, you were marked in him with a seal, the promised Holy Spirit.*" A seal, in Paul's time, was the attestation of a legal signature to declare valid ownership. That is what The Holy Spirit is; it is a seal on believers so that all those who dare look know that they are owned by God. The Holy Spirit is our mark of adoption as God's children. It is His "seal of approval" in that we are given His Spirit to do His will. A seal that is not burned on but given to us to live in us through grace.

The idea of "born again,"...you guessed, comes from the Holy Spirit. Romans 8:10-11 expounds on this as it draws out that it is The Holy Spirit that makes believers "new" and gives them eternal life. Being baptized not by the water but by The Spirit allows us to commune with God and have eternal life. Faith is the retainer agreement; that is what gives The Holy Spirit the authority to help believers in times of struggle, to give them strength, and to intercede on their behalf. *"In the same way, the Spirit helps us in our weakness. We do not know what we ought to pray for, but the Spirit himself intercedes for us through wordless groans. And he who searches our hearts knows the mind of the Spirit because the Spirit intercedes for God's people in accordance with the will of God"* (Romans 8:26-27 NIV).

What Does The Holy Spirit Do? The Holy Spirit teaches, protects, guides, strengthens, saves, changes, gives, judges... basically...The Holy Spirit has made life on this rock a life worth living. You have seen Him at work; you have felt Him.

- 82 -

What makes more sense that a hammer drove a nail or that a hand guided a hammer? Anyone who has spent prolonged periods of time with people, in general, is well aware...we are hammers. The Holy Spirit CAN do all the wonders of God but WILL do as much as you let Him do in your life.

HOW CAN A PERSON GET FILLED WITH THE HOLY SPIRIT?

Just Ask. That is all faith takes. He gives freely to any and all who ask and accept.

Avery: Not everyone can be saved.

Me: Wrong...all can be saved.

Avery: Some things cannot be forgiven.

Me: Wrong again...there is no sin greater than God.

Avery: Not greater than Him, but too big to be forgiven.

Me: If the sin is beyond a God's forgiveness, then it is not much of a god.

Avery: So, you are saying a child murderer and rapist can be forgiven?

Me: Not by me.

Avery: But by God?

Me: Yes.

Avery: Should we really worship a God who can forgive that?

Me: That is the only God worth worshipping, not only because it is the only God, but because He is perfect, and as such, child murder is the same as jaywalking because sin is sin is sin is sin...period...and not a single soul is outside His ability to forgive.

Avery: But why?

Me: Because...He thinks you're worth it.

Avery: How can I worship a God who can forgive evil?

Me: By thanking Him for forgiving yours, and not worrying about if He's forgiving mine...I am more than capable of praying for my own salvation...in time, you can join me... but start with your own.

It really is that simple. To be filled with The Holy Spirit, all you need do is exist. Jesus did the rest. The Spirit resides in you. Like a tap, you need to open it up and let Him flow through you. Accept that He exists, and He does. Talk to Him while sitting in traffic, while having your lunch, tell Him your fears and hopes, tell Him I am sorry for the whole "Hayden" thing...I was just trying to articulate a point. Acknowledge Him throughout your day. Prayer need not be some candle-fueled fire hazard; it can be a sandwich in the parking lot at work. In that prayer is how you get filled with The Holy Spirit. There is no spell or incantation. God is not about magic words; He is about truth. So, if you want to be filled with the Spirit of Truth...Honestly, ask for it.

HOW DO WE RESIST TEMPTATION AND EVIL?

Avery: So, why is there evil in the world?

Me: I honestly don't have the best answer for that.

Avery: And that doesn't bother you?

Me: Faith is not about having all the right answers...it is about trusting that someone else does, even if He doesn't share them.

Avery: I have a hard time accepting a God that allows evil in the world.

Me: And that is OK...you can have a hard time with it. Most things worth doing are not easy.

Avery: So, are you believers less prone to evil than others?

Me: (uncontrollable laughter) You have heard of the Crusades, right?

Avery: Yeah yeah.

Me: Or the entire book of Job?

Avery: Got it.

Me: Or the plight of Moses and the book of Exodus?

Avery: OK…then how do you avoid evil?

Me: You don't…you avoid temptation and fight evil.

Evil exists. That is a cold hard truth. Regardless of your socioeconomic, racial, religious, cultural, etc. background… it exists. Whether it was a relative who had a serial number tattooed on them during World War Two, a friend who lives with shrapnel imbedded in their flesh because of a suicide bomber, or yourself who has been used, unappreciated, and abused by those who claim to love you, nobody is immune to the reach and infection of evil in our lives.

What is evil? Like Justice Stewart Potter once so famously said, "I know it when I see it." We know examples, and we can identify them, but what is evil? Synonyms for evil are: wicked, bad, wrong, immoral, sinful, and ungodly. That last one is the one I am going to focus on for a moment… *ungodly*. The absence of God. To me, that is the most terrifying concept in the existence of all realities. Yet, I take comfort in knowing that nothing exists outside of God. So, the question then becomes how I reconcile the existence of evil with the existence of an all-powerful and loving God. Well, that is an amazing question.

Evil personified has many names. Satan, Devil, Beelzebub, Mephistopheles, Iblis, or Lucifer…take your pick. "The Prince of Darkness" is a popular title, and I think a good one. Hiding in the shadows, unseen, whispering lies and hate, creating doubt, and spreading fear. Yet, still just a prince. If you have ever seen a Barn Owl take flight, or the bloom of a Dragon Fruit Flower, or the bright glow of stars on a moonless night in the countryside...then you know that God is in the dark. Mr. Mephistopheles, or whatever he's calling himself these days, maybe the Prince of darkness, but the beauty and assurance that comes with faith is knowing who The King is. Evil has no dominion, no ownership, no rights; it simply interferes and tempts us.

The best explanation I ever heard about evil came from the most unlikely source. Not scripture, not a pastor, not family, not a scholar...but from a victim. A 12-year-old sexual assault victim. This kid said to me, "Evil is what happens when hurt just overflows from one person onto another." This kid was assaulted in the most egregious way by someone who was supposed to love and protect them, and instead of holding onto hate and resentment, they were able to process an immeasurable pain with a level of compassion that would make a monk blush. That is how we defeat evil.

The sad truth is that evil is completely unavoidable. You will be faced with evil. You will confront it, and to many, you will embody it. You are the villain in someone's story, and that is just the way sin has infected the world. The utopian answer, and even a Biblical one, is to cut out the infection and not be of this world. Original sin may have occurred in the garden, but we did not stop there. The human capacity for evil is mind-boggling. You cannot turn on the news or listen to the radio or lift a paper without being reminded of the dark and twisted nature of humanity. The stench of sin wafts across the globe, and we choke on it.

So, on that happy note…how can we resist evil if not avoid it? Well, Hayden Smith can help with that.

Man was imbued with The Holy Spirit for more than one reason. One of those reasons would be to combat evil. That is what resistance is. It is an active response to evil. In dealing with evil, we cannot play defense; avoidance will often lead to unwitting surrender and appeasement of evil. "The only thing necessary for the triumph of evil is for good men to do nothing." This quote is often attributed to Edmond Burke, while others say it was John Stuart Mill. Regardless of its origin, the sentiment is on point. A point that is supported biblically in Proverbs 24:11-12 where we are actively told to rescue and save others.

Historically, there has been a debate on morality and evil. Philosophers of Ancient Greece argued whether or not evil actually existed or whether it was simply a manmade concept to deter men from their nature. Such theories have existed as long as men scribbled on walls as they illustrated people butchering one another. The idea that man is inherently evil and that we create these codes of conduct and religious structures to try and quell the insidious nature of ourselves is…well…depressing. People who subscribe to this theory explain the Mother Teresas and Fred Rogers' of the world as nothing more than narcissists who fake goodness to be noticed and feed their internal selfish desire to be known or as the proverbial exceptions to the rule.

Of course, throughout human history, Evil has been personified not just by the Judeo-Christian concept of "Satan." Whiro, the Māori god of darkness and evil, ruler of the underworld. The Māori people believed that any evil actions done by man were, in fact, the work of Whiro. Loviatar is the Finnish goddess of death, pain, and disease; she was described as the blind daughter of Tuoni, the ruler of the underworld. She was believed to be the source of all the ills and plagues. The Ancient Egyptians had their own take on evil personified in Apophis; this god was credited with all darkness, destruction, chaos, and evil in the world. A personal favorite of mine is Lamashtu, the Mesopotamian goddess who preyed on women during childbirth and feasted on newborns. Lilith is without a doubt deserving of an honorable mention here as many Judeo texts describe her as the first bride of Adam, scorned and turned away to become the serpent herself who tempted Eve.

How do we resist evil? Together. You see, this is where religion and faith can get into an epic duel. Biblically we are told to lean on Christ and trust only in Him. True. Yet, we are instructed to seek the counsel of others and love one another. Also, true. Finding the balance is essential to resisting evil. If you have suicidal ideations, pray and seek the Lord above all else, but some people are gifted with healing, knowledge, and discernment; some of them become psychologists, social workers, psychiatrists, therapists, counselors, etc. Seeking help; human help is not a violation of faith. If anything, it is in strict accordance with Proverbs 19:20. The Wisdom of Solomon is renowned, and he is credited with authoring the Book of Proverbs. Be wary of advice that steers you away from The Word...but be just as wary of Zealots who steer you away from help.

People need not be evil to aid evil. I know people of faith who have actively talked persons out of going to rehab because the program was not faith-based. They meant well; they were concerned about the person. They wanted to ensure that the help and advice they received was spiritually appropriate. They meant well, but I attended the person's funeral after they overdosed. There is an old saying, "*the road to hell was paved with good intentions.*" The reason this saying is so old is because of the ring of truth it carries.

The reason evil is so difficult to fight is because it is a choice. This is where religion comes in handy for people. The concept that *the devil made me do it* is very appealing. However, if you've walked through a Holocaust Museum, if you have seen the eyes of a child rapist, or witnessed a man choke a woman because she refused his sexual advances, then you are fully aware that evil is human. Religion provides a scapegoat for evil. Faith does not.

Faith in Christ does not prescribe to the idea that the devil made me do it. Granted, demonic possession and influence are a very real part of the faith. However, prayer and repentance are how we avoid such attacks from the demonic. It is just like that fateful day in the garden. We are faced with a choice. Every moment of every day, we must choose. The decision not to choose is, in fact, a choice, every choice may be the wrong one, but you must make it anyway... that is both the burden and gift of free will. Knowing that people are capable of greatness and evil is what makes Jesus' selfless sacrifice that much more impactful. He went to the cross not just for Fred Rogers but also for Hitler, and that is a really hard pill for us to swallow. Luckily, we don't have to swallow it...He did that too.

So, like I said...how do we resist evil? Together. Together means not just with one another but together with Christ through The Holy Spirit. Evil can be viewed as a jackal in many cultures, I personally think that is a little harsh against the poor animal, but metaphorically we can work with it. A jackal will not attack a strong group or herd; it will seek out the straggler, the sick or weak, the lonely and desperate. The jackal is seeking the one sheep that strayed. Evil is seeking that one. The Good News is that so is He: *What do you think? If a man owns a hundred sheep, and one of them wanders away, will he not leave the ninety-nine on the hills and go to look for the one that wandered off? And if he finds it, truly I tell you, he is happier about that one sheep than about the ninety-nine that did not wander off. In the same way, your Father in heaven is not willing that any of these little ones should perish.* (Matthew 18:12-14 NIV).

So, how do we resist evil? Together with Jesus.

HOW/WHY SHOULD WE TELL OTHERS ABOUT OUR FAITH?

Religious faiths spread throughout time and place through a process that a group of intellectuals determined should be called "diffusion." The interesting thing is that diffusion is a result of countless catalytic events. War, missionary work, natural disasters, etc., all can be credited with the spread of religions.

Islamic diffusion is credited to military conquest and what is considered the historically fair treatment of conquered peoples. Also, there are economic implications to Islamic diffusion over the centuries, as Mecca was a major source of global trade.

Buddhist diffusion has historically been done through relocation diffusion and missionary work, not as rapid as military conquest, but also historically receives better **PR** because of it.

The Crusades and Spanish Inquisition are perhaps some of the more renowned acts of diffusion as they are, without a doubt, not exactly the paradigm on how we should spread The Good News.

Every religion that has ever existed has attempted to spread. The Christian idea of *The Great Commission,* as defined in Matthew 28:16-20 is not distinctly Christian.

Yet, those who live with faith feel this incessant need to share their faith with others, some are more obnoxious than others, but regardless of belief, if there is a belief, a measure of faith, then there is this internal desire to tell others. Why?

If you knew the secret to cure cancer, ending world hunger, stopping pollution, or whatever catastrophe you could think of...if you had that knowledge and kept it to yourself, you would be one of the cruelest human beings to have ever walked this earth. That is why people of faith tend to be so annoying with trying to tell non-believers about their faith; they know the secret to life, how to live forever and be free of pain, suffering, and doubt. Their faith gives them a lens through which they view the world differently, and many would argue more clearly.

Why people share their faith is not really a mystery, it is both a clear directive of many faiths and, more importantly, it is a moral imperative for most people of faith. The mystery becomes how to share one's faith without the pious arrogance that so often comes along with it. We have all met those holier-than-thou types as they "explain" to someone why they are not living rightly. That Bible-toting blue-haired lady who clutches her pearls because you dared to support gay marriage, all the while she had actual cocaine in her soda as a child and refused to share a water fountain with a person of color. Or that man who tells you that your dietary choices are against the will of God, but he beats his wife or kids. The issue that comes with the sharing of faith is that the delivery vessel is imperfect yet attempts to proffer a message of pure perfection. Basically, a bag of trash is not the best delivery method for priceless jewels.

Back to that quote, we will for argument sake just assume it was William Thom who said it; "be careful how you live; you will be the only Bible some people ever read."

1 Timothy 4:16 CSB was written long before William Thoms' dad was ever conceived; it says, *"Pay close attention to your life and your teaching; persevere in these things, for by doing this you will save both yourself and your hearers."*

The idea of leading by example is one that we impress upon our children. We tell them not to lower themselves. We expect them to approach things with a level of responsibility and character that we adults regularly fail to exhibit. If you tell Christians that they should not judge others, they will whip out John 7:24 like it is a shootout in the wild west; yet most miss the point. Righteous Judgment does not mean we get to chastise or punish because we must recognize that we are not righteous. We are of this world despite any efforts not to be. We are sinners and fall short of the Glory that stands in righteous judgment. Hence, Matthew 7:1-2.

Avery: Do you think you have the right to judge someone who is gay?

Me: I guess it depends on what I am judging them for.

Avery: They're gay.

Me: OK.

Avery: So, can you judge them?

Me: For what?

Avery: For being gay.

Me: Oh…sounds like you certainly have.

Christians can be *judgy*. The truth is, we cannot help it; we feel the need to correct sinful behavior. Any Christian that is complicit with sinful behavior and life choices needs to really reexamine what it means to be a Christian because, in truth, we are called to repel sin and save all our brothers and sisters from sin while also respecting the idea of free will, it's a fun balancing act. However, finesse is needed. People love to point out the John 2:15-16 story of Jesus brandishing a whip and flipping tables. The New Testament is comprised of 27 books, and Jesus flipping tables is one paragraph. Feeding the poor, healing the blind and lame, loving on those who are unworthy…that's most of the book. Jesus could flip tables because He stood in righteousness, me, you, anyone else alive on earth right now…not so much. So, the question then is how do we spread our faith and address sin without being too obnoxious? Luckily, the instruction manual has a pretty easy-to-understand directive in 1 Corinthians 16:14. A verse so important to me that it is inscribed in my wedding ring and mounted on the wall of my house, not because of my piety, but because I am a sinful trash bag that needs the reminder. Regardless of your translation of choice, the message is a simple one.

New International Version:

Do everything in love.

New Living Translation:

And do everything with love.

English Standard Version:

Let all that you do be done in love.

Berean Study Bible:

Do everything in love.

Berean Literal Bible:

Let all things of you be done in love.

King James Bible:

Let all your things be done with charity.

New King James Version::

Let all that you do be done with love.

New American Standard Bible

All that you do must be done in love.

Amplified Bible::

Let everything you do be done in love [motivated and inspired by God's love for us].

Christian Standard Bible

Do everything in love.

Holman Christian Standard Bible:

Your every action must be done with love.

American Standard Version:

Let all that ye do be done in love.

Aramaic Bible in Plain English:

And let all your dealings be with love.

Contemporary English Version:

Show love in everything you do.

Douay-Rheims Bible:

Let all your things be done in charity.

Good News Translation:

Do all your work in love.

International Standard Version:

Everything you do should be done lovingly.

Literal Standard Version:

Let all your things be done in love.

New American Bible:

Your every act should be done with love.

NET Bible:

Everything you do should be done in love.

New Revised Standard Version:

Let all that you do be done in love.

New Heart English Bible:

Let all that you do be done in love.

Weymouth New Testament:

Let all that you do be done from motives of love.

World English Bible:

Let all that you do be done in love.

Young's Literal Translation:

Let all your things be done in love.

Pretty easy to understand but practically impossible to follow. However, that is the key. That is how we spread our Faith. My conversations with Avery were at times heated, and yet, we had a level of mutual respect for one another; I have a love for Avery, and Avery has a love for me...it is through that love that this literary drivel has made it to your eyes...that is how we spread our faith. We love one another. If someone hurts and betrays you...love them. In Abraham Lincoln's inaugural address, he said, "We are not enemies, but friends. We must not be enemies. Though passion may have strained, it must not break our bonds of affection. The mystic chords of memory will swell when again touched, as surely they will be by the better angels of our nature." I am not The Apostle Paul or the great orator that Abraham Lincoln was. I turn to Tina Turner when dealing with people I do not like as "What's love got to do, got to do with it" echoes through my brain...hence the inscribed ring.

So, why do we tell others of our faith...because we should.

So, how do we tell others of our faith...lovingly.

IS THERE STILL HEALING TODAY?

Avery: Why childhood cancer?

Me: I don't know.

Avery: Why do healthy 30-year-olds have heart attacks?

Me: I don't know.

Avery: Why does God heal some and not others?

Me: I honestly have no idea.

Avery: Seems kinda cruel, doesn't it?

Me: It certainly does come across that way.

Let me be perfectly clear. I will not hide behind *"Everything happens for a reason"* or *"It is all part of God's plan."* When I said, "I honestly have no idea," ...I meant it. I do not have those answers. I have stood at the casket of a child as tears streamed down my face. I have held the grieving wife of a man lost in his youth. I have sat with my father as he clutched a vial of ground-up bones that was once his son. I genuinely have no idea why I had to deal with any of that.

I sat with a woman who went for a scan to find that the cancer had gone. I watched my mother walk out of a hospital after seeing a car that nobody should've left alive. I listened to a colleague explain to me that his son's doctor had to run more tests because it appeared that his heart had healed itself.

The truth is that God does still heal people. We have all heard the tales of miraculous and unexplained healings. We have seen people laying hands and praying over the sick and afflicted. We have also seen people exploit the ill and prey on them. It is seemingly without any rhyme or reason. There appears to be no order in who receives healing and who does not.

We scroll through social media and see *Can Little Timmy Get 1,000 Likes So He Can Be Healed* or a photo of someone in a hospital bed that says *Most Will Just Scroll Past, Those Who Believe Will Comment "AMEN" So Timmy Can Be Healed.* What is that all about? God is not scrolling social media. Jesus does not count Your followers. Grace and Healing from God are not achieved through popularity contests. They are not earned through acts of faith either, as there are countless believers who suffer illness and die horrible and painful deaths. Nobody can give you a proper explanation. Faith is not about having all the answers; it is about living with the questions knowing that He does have all the answers.

The healing nature of God is not always so easily seen. We live in a miraculous existence, so we often miss the miracles.

We are used to them. The hands of Dr. Ben Carson have performed miraculous surgeries. The brilliance of John Eccles as he tirelessly worked in the fields of Physiology and Medicine. Francis Collins' research on the Human Genome Project as it made huge strides in genetic medicine. Gregor Mendel, the 19th Century Abbot, considered by many to be the father of genetics. Sophie Brahe, with her advances in medicine. Miriam Stimson played a huge role in the development of understanding DNA. God used all of them to advance scientific and medical research for the health and welfare of humankind. All of them are miracle workers, along with countless others.

GOD STILL HEALS TODAY. That choice of font and typeface is purposeful. Before we go any further, we must acknowledge that God does, in fact, heal. The word "still" is indicative that historically people have been more open to accepting the healings of God. There was a time when the healing power of God was not questioned. It was sought and accepted. The irony is that the more miracles we as a people became witness to, the less we seem to notice them. Scripture is filled with miraculous examples, from natural phenomena to healings and resurrections. The majesty of The Grand Canyon, the splendor of the Aurora borealis, the magnificence of Victoria Falls, or the simple act of a bumblebee flying...miracles in nature are all around us.

The fact that you exist right now is against mathematical odds; forty million cells storming one other cell in a biological maze, the perfect combination of which is required to make up your specific genetic code...miracle. The fact that part of this book was written on a tablet that is charged wirelessly and transmits electronic communications through the air... miracle. The fact that men walked on the moon less than a century after the first motor vehicle was made is a miracle. Finding your soulmate... a miracle. Childbirth...miracle. Yet, in an age of massive technological advances, we tend to scoff at the miraculous nature of our everyday lives. We walk around with our earbuds, smartphones, Bluetooth, and digitally assisted wireless lives and perform tasks that our not-too-distant ancestors would have considered witchcraft. Yet, we quickly disregard the fact that this knowledge and ability is divinely given.

We do not give credit to God where it is due. However, we have no problem blaming Him or resenting Him when things do not go as planned...as we planned. We find it easy to fault God for those who are not healed. How can we justify that? Those who suffer a devastating loss understandably turn to anger with God. Being angry with God is healthy (at this point, my Pastor and Holy Roller friends are cursing the book and praying for me, some in tongues). If you are angry with God, you have a relationship with God. As He understands us better than we do, He accepts the anger. He absorbs the hate. He hears the complaints, He lives with the resentment, and He returns all of that with love, patience, understanding, and grace.

This section is short because the answer is simply "yes." Yes, God still heals today. Yet, beyond that, I have no answers.

Avery: How can you pray to a God that allows children to suffer and die?

Me: Quietly and with fear and awe.

Avery: So, you fear God?

Me: Absolutely...you know, if you search "fear of God" online, you will see shoes, hoodies, and clothing lines before you find anything remotely Judeo-Christian.

Avery: Really?

Me: yes...because people do not understand that the fear of God is a beautiful thing, it is an intimate thing of awe and wonder...we have all heard the adage that we "fear what we do not understand"...well...nothing is less understandable than God.

Avery: Then why worship Him...Her...It?

Me: I worship God because I cannot answer your questions.

Avery: What?

Me: ...I don't know why children suffer and die, or why some people are barren, or others contract terrible sicknesses while rapists and murderers live long healthy lives...I know that to God, murder and impure thoughts are the same things because He is the epitome of perfection, and wrong is wrong. I worship God because there is so much that I cannot answer and do not know, but I know Him, and to know an unknowable God is a great feeling.

WHY GO TO CHURCH?

Avery: So, do you have to go to Church to believe in God?

Me: Do I?...Absolutely.

Avery: You know what I mean.

Me: There are many people who attend Church and probably have absolutely no faith whatsoever.

Avery: Then why would they go?

Me: They think that's where they may be able to get some.

Avery: I guess that is not a bad place to start.

Me: Or an absolutely terrible place.

Church is not a place. There are a bunch of huggers who wear shirts that indicate "Be the Church." There are plenty of Christians who lean into the Song Of Solomon and proudly exclaim that they are "The Bride." Both are right, and both are probably going somewhere on their selected day of Sabbath. For our purposes, let's keep it simple and say "Sunday"...really...that's between you and God.

The idea that we are "The Church" is an important and accurate one. Just not a very helpful one. We are all parts of the same body, I have met my fair share of "less desirable parts" on this earth, but the point is that we all have something to contribute. That is right out of 1 Corinthians 12. The Church of Corinth is believed to be founded by Paul, yes that Paul who we've called a major contributor to what is commonly known as "The Bible." Yet, just like any Church, it had its problems of misplaced superiority, sexual scandals, questionable financial practices, and a slew of other issues. Since the inception of "The Church." There have been issues.

I mean the inception, long before Christ walked this earth. Human sacrifices are prehistoric in nature. All records of all ancient societies indicate some spiritual or religious institutions, practices, and gatherings. Temples of Ancient Greece and Egypt are swarmed with tourists to this day. Organized religion exists because it draws people in. They find something attractive about it. So, why do we still *go to church*?

Fellowship. First and foremost, we corporately meet so that we can meet corporately. We are social beings; we were designed that way. Those Sunday gatherings are so that we can come together for our intended purpose, to spend time together in celebration and peace, and to experience joy and freedom in our fellowship. We, Us, Our...let me be unequivocally clear, I don't just mean fellowship of Jew and Gentile. It's not just like-minded friends getting together. This fellowship is between us and the Creator of the cosmos. Sunday gatherings give us an opportunity to enjoy fellowship with God. The Creator of heaven and earth yearns to spend time with and rest with us. That is the core of *going to church.*

Worship music...prayer...speaking in tongues...loud exaltation...preaching...laughter...etc. Whatever it looks like, any church that ministers to the heart of God is fulfilling its primary purpose. That is why Adam was made and why everyone since has been made. We go to church because it is natural for us to do so.

Church is a collection of people, and at my ripe age, I have learned one indisputable truth. People are disappointing. Luckily God goes beyond our disappointments and shrouds us in an inexplicable amount of grace. I have asked several Church leaders, priests, pastors, etc., this question, but none have been comfortable answering it. *Which of the seven letters is your church getting?*

The letters refer to the letters included in the Book of Revelation, the last Book of the Bible. A book shrouded in much mystery and imagery, terrifying and confusing to many, inspirational and moving to those who take the time to appreciate it. The book itself is transcribed by John, an actual follower of Christ, during his ministry here on earth. A fisherman who, as a result of his work with Jesus and subsequent works, was banished to the island of Patmos, where he transcribed the Book of Revelation and the seven letters to seven churches that are contained within that book. Transcribed...I have used that word twice now. Why? Words have meaning; John makes it clear that the source of the book, the true author, is Jesus (Revelation 1:1-2).

The Church of Ephesus is the first Church to get a letter. Ephesus was a major trade city in Asia at the time. The church there prided itself on all of its hard work and for its rejection of false prophets (Revelation 2:2-3). Yet, it is Revelation 2:4 that is the core of this letter. Despite their good works, doctrine, and perseverance, this Church was identified by Jesus as a Church that had forsaken the love of Christ and His teachings. Truth and love are symbiotic in true Christianity. The Church of Ephesus and many today herald their moral superiority and doctrinal compliance at the expense of love. Jesus is love. He teaches us that we must teach Truth in Love, not in hate or judgment.

The second letter is awarded to the Church of Smyrna. Not the most popular Church. Poor and small, highly persecuted. This church was not admonished by Christ but rather warned. They were warned of wrongful persecution and imprisonment, even to the point of death, yet, they were promised the "crown of life" (Revelation 2:10 ESV). Christians are still persecuted, and I don't mean with shows they don't like and clothing they disagree with...I mean real persecution, torture, and death around the world because of their faith. These Christians may not be in the pew next to you, but they are our brothers and sisters, and they are suffering for their faith. They are loved, and we as a Church must stand with them and remember the eternal reward that awaits the faithful.

The third letter, and one I believe more churches today would receive than they would like to admit, is the letter to Pergamum. Pergamum was a city known for its pagan rituals. Jesus applauds the Church for maintaining their faith despite these pagan influences, but then He addresses their sin. This church's sin is in their compromise. In order to maintain peaceful and healthy existence, they compromise their beliefs and convictions. This is all too prevalent today. Churches will normalize non-Christian behavior and, at times, embrace sinful existence. We are told not to conform but to be transformed (Romans 12:2). Too many Churches focus on attendance and financial viability and compromise the teachings of Christ in order to keep the lights on. This letter, coupled with the first, shows us the extremes of today's churches.

The next letter was addressed to Thyatira. A wealthy city with great commerce and trade, lauded for its growing service. Yet, this church devoted itself to the teachings of false prophets. Idolatry leads to immorality, and Jesus himself reminds the congregants that even if the false prophet remains unrepentant that the body of the church can be saved by His grace if they repent. Jesus is just and fair. We get what we deserve...that should be terrifying because as we know, the payment for sin is death, yet grace has us covered. There are so many charismatic speakers, teachers, and talking heads that we are subjected to today.

It is easy to get dragged into false teachings; the key is to walk away. A Church that exalts the speaker over the message is a church you should promptly leave. I was in a church recently that had Luke 4:7 painted on their wall with flowers and butterflies around it. I quickly put my jacket on and left. The best way to avoid false prophets is to follow the word and know who speaks what words (look it up).

The fifth letter went to Sardis. In my opinion, this is the saddest letter; all the letters' admonishments can be traced to acts of wrongdoing. Here is a church that just fell spiritually dead. The city was a war-torn city, and Christ uses this fact in explaining to the congregants that they need to "wake up" as He alludes to sneak attacks that had plagued the city. He mentions that those who repent will be dressed in victors' gowns. Ritualistic and scheduled prayer, Bible studies, Ministry outreaches, all of these are great works...but work alone, you know. Churches today can easily wither on the vine and become zombies without even knowing it. If Jesus is not in your church...it is not a church.

The letter to Philadelphia echoes the sentiment of that of Smyrna's letter. The city was not known for its loving acceptance of Christians, and Christ again promised His followers to keep the faith even as they faced persecution and trials. This Church was not known for its resources or strength, yet He promised His protection. This letter should be burned into the hearts of Christians. Regardless of our shortcomings, we will persevere through faith in Him.

The final letter is to Laodicea. Another wealthy city with a prosperous Church where Jesus states He is about to "spit [them] out of [His] mouth" (see Revelation 3:16 NIV). Ouch. The Church here is described and chastised for their lukewarm faith. Neither hot nor cold, this Church just is. We see these Churches everywhere today, the Churches that are so focused on financial prosperity and community involvement. They boast of their donations and charities, advertise their programs, and have great mission statements and active social media accounts. He appeals to this Church's desire to have spiritual wealth because that is what we all truly yearn for.

So...what letter is your Church getting?

What letter are you getting?

These are questions you should address before finding a Church to call "home," which is ironic since the Church I currently attend is called "Home Church." They are not a perfect Church, there are fellow congregants I don't particularly like, and I dare say even more who do not particularly like me, and that is OK. Church is a family, and I have plenty of family who I avoid at all costs. At my Church, I have two lead Pastors. One said they hoped they would get the Smyrna letter...and the other said they thought it was possible they would get the letter to Laodicea...both love their Church and are fully connected and committed to serving the Lord. Both have different personal experiences and relationships with their Church, and *THAT* is why you should attend Church.

Avery: If I wanted to go to Church, I wouldn't even know where to begin.

Me: I guess that depends on why you want to go.

Avery: I guess to find God.

Me: Whoa…I had no idea He was missing.

Here is something that almost no Church Leader will openly say: Church is not where you go to "find God." Church is where you go to worship God and spend time with Him and grow in your relationship with Him. To find God, go to the beach, hike in the woods, hold your kid, sit with your spouse, and take some time to pray. God is there in your yearning. Finding God is not difficult; that's kind of the beauty of omnipresence. Recognizing God… is the key. This is not to say that you should avoid Church if you are questioning, struggling, or doubting your faith. If something is telling you to go to Church, go. That "something" is Hayden Smith (I know, you thought that silly moniker was done). He is there in the yearning. If you are yearning, don't ignore it.

Finding the Church that is right for you is done the same way you find the right shoes: know your size, your style, and try them on…with socks.

Knowing your size, do you like to be hugged, greeted, or bombarded with emails and friend requests? Do you want programs, plans, and social activities? Do you want services in Latin and ritualistic practices? Do you want pews or drum circles? Knowing your size means just that, knowing how involved you want to be in your Church and how involved you want your Church to be in you. I love my Pastors and consider them friends; we have had some uncomfortable conversations as only real family can have. I love people who have left the Church I attend, but they are still very much part of My Church because they are my family; they fit me. Know what you want from Church and what you can give; know your size.

Know your style. This is where denominations and worship are important. I was raised Catholic. I was baptized as a baby and went through my sacraments; that was the Church of my youth. As an adult, I've been baptized twice at two separate Churches. The first time was to feel closer to my blood family, and it was done in grief. The second time was done in a half-inflated pool on Main Street as I was dunked by a man I used to watch play sports on the fields of my High School. That time I got more than wet; I was filled with the living waters they talk about in the good book. I have preached at Lutheran Church, I have preached at a few Catholic Churches, I have preached at a Baptist Church, and a Nondenominational Christian Church. I even preached at Pentecostal Church and a Protestant Church. None of those Churches were "wrong" for me; I was just not right for them. It just was not my style.

Trying them on; just go. Going to Church is the best way to determine if going to Church is right for you. If you're uncomfortable, that doesn't mean it's the wrong Church for you...quite the opposite. Why are you uncomfortable? Being convicted and moved can be a good thing. Surgery is not comfortable. Detox is not comfortable. Therapy is not comfortable. Rehabilitation is not comfortable. Comfort is not the point; salvation is. If you are immediately comfortable, ask why. Is it because this feels like family, or is it because there is no conviction...very different kinds of comfort...and you should have very different reactions. Try a few Churches; if you are looking for a Church, the truth is that a Church is looking for you too.

With socks...a terrible metaphor, but at this point, I'm committed. Many households have you remove your shoes upon entering for purposes of cleanliness. Many cultures have you remove your shoes upon entering a home, restaurant, and, most significantly...a place of worship for respect, comfort, and reverence. Exodus 3:5 is one of my favorite moments in scripture. God tells Moses to stop in his tracks and remove his sandals because he is standing on holy ground. Unknown to my pastors, I have often removed my shoes in worship...and my Church is in a tent, outside, with rocks and ants and stuff...hence...socks. When finding a Church, be prepared to be unprepared...you may find yourself on Holy Ground.

Avery: I just don't know if I could ever feel comfortable walking into a Church.

Me: I sure hope not.

Avery: What?

Me: Imagine walking through a park with your dog, and you come across a single bush in a clearing engulfed in flames and speaking to you.

Avery: OK.

Me: Do you think you would be comfortable?

Avery: Absolutely not.

Me: Well...that was emphatic.

"Absolutely not," Avery here gave us an elimination of doubt. Ironic, isn't it? This phrase indicates strong disagreement and is usually stated as an interjection. People tend to interject this statement when they must impart their discomfort or disagreement with the proffered situation. The church is not about comfort. Being in the presence of God is meant to be awe-inspiring, not commonplace. Grabbing your coffee and singing along with worship may be a fun way to start the week, but that is not going to Church. Reading specific scripture, saying certain prayers, and listening to a great preacher give a moving sermon are all wonderful ways to grow in your faith and strengthen your bond with fellow believers and even with God, but it is not going to Church. Going to Church is quite easy; just go to Him, be with Him and experience worship and corporately celebrate your relationship with God, whatever that relationship is.

Avery: So, can I come to Church with you?

Me: Of course, you can.

Avery: What if I feel like I don't belong?

Me: You think that's bad?...wait til you feel like you do.

AVERY'S LETTER

If I am completely honest, I have no idea what to say. I don't have any answers. In fact, since my talks with Joe, I have only had more questions. I attended an ALPHA Course with him and developed great relationships and friendships. As cliché as it sounds, one of them was with God.

I still don't know what it means to be a believer, and I am not sure I am what most people would think of as a Christian. All I know is that I feel better and more complete. My marriage is better. My work life is more productive. I'm happier and healthier, and the only real difference is that I opened myself to the possibility of there being a God.

I was a devout Atheist, which is to say that I believed in a void. Some atheists simply do not believe in God; they believe in perfect chaos without explanation. Then there was me, the angry atheist who actively believed in nothingness and was furious at those who had faith. I was angry because I had a void, and they didn't. They had filled their void with unicorns, fairies, and a make-believe man in the clouds who played games with our lives. A bearded guy in a tunic who killed my loved ones without provocation or explanation, and they worshipped him happily. So, when Joe invited me to his ALPHA, I was furious; I respected this guy's intellect, yet he was a Christian. I declined his invitation and instead insulted him viciously, and he responded by taking me to lunch, over and over and over again. I know you're just reading this, but I must explain something. Joe is not that nice. I have watched him make people cry and be annoyed by their sensitivity. He is not nice, but he is a good man, and he saw through my insults and anger. He saw a pain that I denied.

I think you should hear one of the conversations that didn't make the cut. It was edited out of the main text, presumably for my benefit; it was our *What's in a Name* conversation. Joe told me the history of Saul, a prominent Jew who expertly convicted Christian zealots, a history I found relatable. Then he told me of the road to Damascus, of the plight of Ananias, and Saul's conversion to Christianity, and how Saul became Paul. Then he went on to explain that Paul wrote Galatians, Romans, Corinthians, Philippians, and Ephesians, and then went on a very boring explanation of how Timothy and Titus are wrongfully attributed to him and how upset that makes him.

Along my road to Damascus came Joe's plight, and apparently, I became "Avery."

I still have questions and doubts, and I now know that is normal. I still have fear, pain, and anxiety, but I now have someplace and someone to turn to with it.

Joe: If you could have any prayer answered, what would it be?

Me: I guess I would want to know if God was real.

Well, my prayer has been answered, and He is real.

My prayer for you is that you question God. Wonder. Press in. Doubt because that invites Him in, and everything will change once you let Him in.

CONCLUSION

So, I made no promises, and I think I delivered on that. I have no great insight into the human condition, nor would I profess to be some grand Christian. I suppose I should've started with this, but ending with it is just as good. To steal from the confession of Maewyn Succat, commonly known as St. Patrick...*I am Joe; I am a sinner, a simple person, and the least of all believers. I am looked down upon by many.* I paraphrase, but that is how St. Patrick started his "Confessio," a writing intended to defend against claims made against him. Still, it is a raw examination of his faith and relationship with Christ. I am no St. Patrick, yet, I hope the few pages preceding this one helped you examine faith and your relationship with God. Ask your questions. Have your doubts. None of us is perfect. That's the point of the cross.

David was an adulterer and a murderer.

Solomon was a money-hungry womanizer.

Abraham was really old...like REALLY old.

Moses was doubtful and had a stutter.

Job was a bankrupt failure.

Noah was a drunk.

Elijah was a suicidal mess.

Peter denied Christ three times, once to his face.

Zacchaeus was greedy.

Paul persecuted Christians.

So many faith institutions focus on "love" and "acceptance." The core of Christianity is a true love, which is not one of simple acceptance but instead of radical transformation. When a preacher says, "Come as you are," that is an invitation not to stay that way but to come that way. All are welcome to faith; all the people above came to God and radically changed. Jesus was so keen on showing radical transformation that he actually changed people's names.

Now I am not saying that you need to change your name; legally, it is a lot of paperwork and a headache, plus there are all these fees. I am saying that you should not fear change, do not fear new.

God loves you, and if you are unsure that God exists…the good news is that God loves you anyway.

If you are pristine, perfect, and righteous in all ways, then I am sorry to have wasted your time. If you are a sinner, a mess at times, and unsure…then I hope something in these pages helped you.

Jesus answered them, "It is not the healthy who need a doctor, but the sick. I have not come to call the righteous, but sinners to repentance" – Luke 5:31-32 NIV.

Prayer is more than a wish list to an invisible man in the clouds. Prayer is genuine communication with a God that loves you. So, when you're done with this…which I assure you is coming soon…just put it down and pray. The worst that happens is you have a few minutes of peace. The best…your life is radically and supernaturally changed for eternity.

I am no great writer (at this point, you have undoubtedly picked up on that)…and I have no idea how to end this book, so I will simply end it with a period.

Milton Keynes UK
Ingram Content Group UK Ltd.
UKHW011927140823
426877UK00002B/27